Microwave

100 MICROWAVE SECRETS

Compiled by Judith Ferguson and Cecilia Norman
Recipes Tested and Prepared by Jacqueline Bellefontaine
Photography by Peter Barry
Designed by Philip Clucas MSIAD
Produced by David Gibbon, Gerald Hughes
    and Ted Smart

CLB 1846
© 1987 Colour Library Books Ltd., Guildford, Surrey, England.
Text filmsetting by Focus Photoset Ltd., London, England.
Printed and bound in Barcelona, Spain by Cronion, S.A.
All rights reserved.
1987 edition published by Crescent Books.
Distributed by Crown Publishers, Inc.
ISBN 0 517 64363 4

h g f e d c b a

Acknowledgement
Microwave ovens used for testing and preparation for
photography supplied by Samsung Electronics (UK) Ltd.
Cookware and accessories provided by Lakeland Plastics
of Windermere, Cumbria. Pyrex and microwave cookware
dishes supplied by Corning Ltd.

Microwave
100 MICROWAVE SECRETS

CRESCENT BOOKS
NEW YORK

Contents

INTRODUCTION

People are usually of two minds about microwave ovens: experienced cooks are sceptical while inexperienced cooks are mystified. Most people who don't own one think a microwave oven is an expensive luxury. Those of us who have one, though, would find it difficult to give it up. Great advances have been made in the design and capabilities of microwave ovens since the demand for them first began in the Sixties. But whether you are an advanced cook or just a beginner, it helps to understand what makes a microwave oven work.

The energy that makes fast cooking possible is comprised of electromagnetic waves converted from electricity. Microwaves are a type of high frequency radio wave. The waves are of short length, hence the name microwave.

Inside the oven is a magnetron, which converts ordinary electricity into microwaves. A wave guide channels the microwaves into the oven cavity, and a stirrer fan circulates them evenly. Microwaves are attracted to the particles of moisture that form part of any food. As the microwaves are absorbed, to a depth of about 1½-2 inches, they cause the water molecules in the food to vibrate about 2000 million times a second. This generates the heat that cooks the food. The heat reaches the center of the food by conduction, just as in ordinary cooking. However, this is accomplished much faster than in conventional cooking because no heat is generated until the waves are absorbed by the food. All the energy is concentrated on cooking the food and not on heating the oven itself or the baking dishes. Standing time is often necessary to allow the food to continue cooking after it is removed from the oven.

Most microwave ovens have an ON indicator light and a timer control. Some timer controls look like minute timers, while others are calibrated in seconds up to 50 seconds and minutes up to 30 minutes. This can vary slightly; some models have a 10 minute interval setting. Some ovens have a separate ON-OFF switch, while others switch on with the timer or power setting. Almost all have a bell or buzzer to signal the end of cooking time.

Cooking times will vary according to the wattage of the oven. The terms used for the different settings also vary from oven to oven.

Power Setting Comparison Chart

	Other Terms and Wattages	Uses
Low	One or two, keep warm, 25%, simmer, defrost. 50-300 watts.	Keeping food warm. Softening butter, cream cheese and chocolate. Heating liquid to dissolve yeast. Gentle cooking.
Medium	Three-six, 40-75% medium low, medium high, stew, braise, roast, reheat, 400-500 watts.	Roasting meat and poultry. Stewing and braising less tender cuts of meat. Baking cakes and custards. Cooking hollandaise sauces.
High	Seven, full, roast, bake, normal, 100%. 550-700 watts	Quick cooking. Meats, fish, vegetables, cookies, pasta, rice, breads, pastry, desserts.

Altering Times

If your oven is not 700W, convert timings in the following way:

500W oven – Add 40 seconds for each minute stated in the recipe.

600W oven – Add 20 seconds for each minute stated in the recipe.

650W oven – Only a slight increase in the overall time is necessary.

Some ovens come equipped with a temperature probe which allows you to cook food according to its internal temperature instead of by time. It is most useful for roasting large cuts of meat. The probe needle is inserted into the thickest part of the food and the correct temperature set on the attached control. When that internal temperature is reached, the oven automatically turns off, or switches to a low setting to keep the food warm. Special microwave thermometers are also available to test internal temperature and can be used inside the oven. Conventional thermometers must never be used inside a microwave oven.

A cooking guide is a feature on some ovens, either integrated into the control panel or on the top or side of the oven housing. It is really a summary of the information found in the instruction and recipe booklet that accompanies every oven. However, it does act as a quick reference and so can be a time saver.

Weights and Measures

LIQUID				DRY	
Metric	Imperial	American		Metric	Imperial
30ml	1 fl oz	2 tbsps		30g	1oz
60ml	2 fl oz	4 tbsps/¼ cup		60g	2oz
90ml	3 fl oz	5 tbsps/⅓ cup		90g	3oz
140ml	¼ pint	½ cup		120g	4oz/¼ lb
280ml	½ pint	1 cup		180g	6oz
430ml	¾ pint	1½ cups		225g	8oz/½ lb
570ml	1 pint	2 cups/16 fl oz		250g	9oz
700ml	1¼ pints	2½ cups		340g	12oz/¾ lb
850ml	1½ pints	3 cups		400g	14oz
1 litre	1¾ pints	3½ cups		450g	1lb
1150ml	2 pints	4 cups		560g	1¼ lbs
				675g	1½ lbs
				790g	1¾ lbs
				900g	2lbs
				1kg	2¼ lbs

Turntables eliminate the need for rotating baking dishes during cooking, although when using a square loaf dish you may need to change its position from time to time anyway. Turntables are usually glass or ceramic and can be removed for easy cleaning. Of all the special features available in microwave ovens, turntables are one of the most useful.

Certain ovens have one or more shelves so that several dishes can be accommodated at once. Microwave energy is

Facing page: (from left to right) a microwave thermometer, conventional meat probe for use outside the oven, and a temperature probe that automatically switches off the oven once preset temperature has been reached are useful accessories for your microwave.

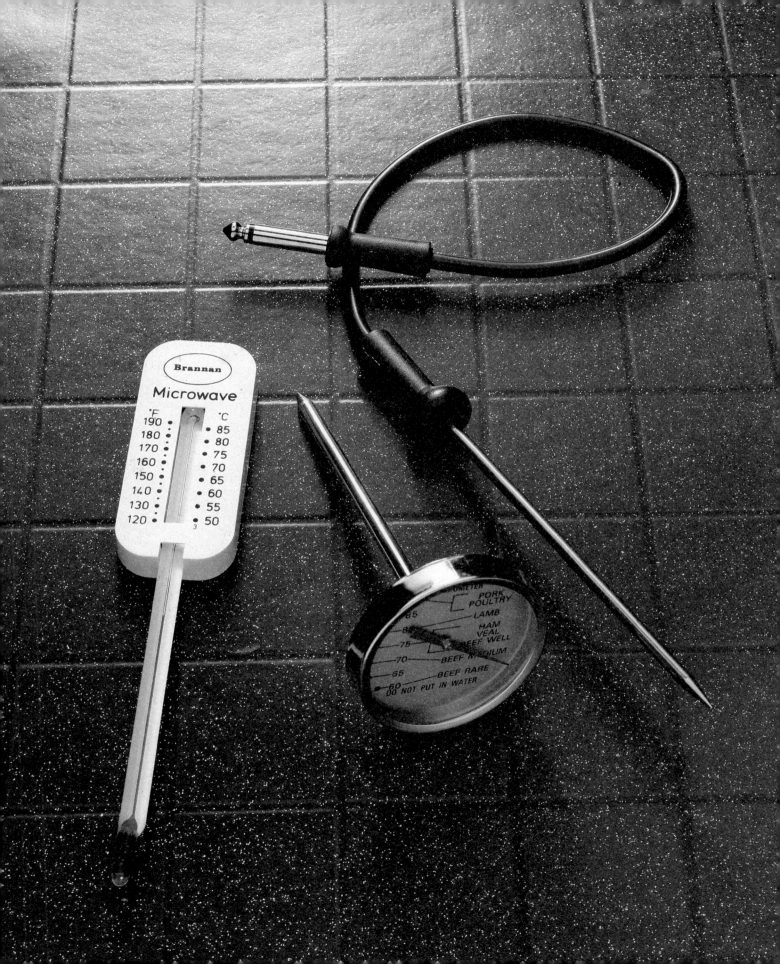

Facing page: a selection of materials suitable for wrapping or covering food, including a handy plastic cover with adjustable steam vent. This page: hot food heats up baking dishes, so always use oven gloves.

higher at the top of the oven than on the floor, and the more you cook at once the longer it all takes. However, these ovens accommodate larger baking dishes than those with turntables.

If you do a lot of entertaining, then an oven with a KEEP WARM setting is a good choice. These ovens have a very low power setting that can keep food warm, without further cooking, for up to one hour. If you want to program your oven like a computer, choose one with a memory control that can switch settings automatically during the cooking cycle.

Browning elements are now available in microwave ovens. They look and operate in much the same way as conventional electric broilers, and if you already have a broiler, you probably don't need a browning element. Some ovens allow the browning element to be used at the same time as the microwave setting, which is a plus.

Combination ovens seem to be the answer to the problem of browning in a microwave oven. While the power settings go by different names in different models, generally there is a setting for microwave cooking alone, a convection setting with conventional electric heat and a setting which combines the two for almost the speed of microwave cooking with the browning ability of convection heat. However, the wattage is usually lower than in standard microwave ovens, and so cooking time will be slightly longer.

On combination settings, use recipes developed for microwave ovens, but follow the instructions with your particular oven for times and settings. Some ovens have various temperature settings to choose from. Breads, poultry, meat and pastries brown beautifully in these ovens, and conventional baking dishes, even metal ones, can be used with a special insulating mat. Beware of certain plastics as they can melt in a combination oven.

Safety and Cleaning

One of the questions most commonly asked is "Are microwave ovens safe to use?". They are safe because they have safety features built into them, and they go through rigorous testing by the manufacturers and by independent agencies.

If you look at a number of microwave ovens you will see that the majority of them are lined with metal, and metal will not allow microwaves to pass through. The doors have special seals to keep the microwaves inside the oven and have cut-out devices to cut off microwave energy immediately the door is opened. There are no pans to upset, no open flames or hot elements and the interior of the oven stays cool enough to touch.

Although microwave ovens don't heat baking dishes, the heat generated by the cooking food does, so it is a good idea to use oven gloves or pot holders to remove dishes from the oven.

It is wise periodically to check the door of your oven to make sure it has not been bent. Check latches and hinges, too, to make sure thay are in good working order. Don't use baking dishes that are too large to allow the turntable to rotate freely; this can cause the motor to over-heat or cause dents in the oven sides and door, lowering efficiency and affecting safety of operation.

Microwave ovens are cleaner and more hygienic to cook with than conventional gas and electric ovens. Foods do not spatter as much and spills do not burn, so clean-up is faster. The turntables and shelves can be removed for easier cleaning. Use non-abrasive cleansers and scrubbers, and be sure to wipe up any residue so that it does not build up around the door seals. Faster cooking times and lower electricity consumption combine to make microwave ovens cheaper to run than conventional ovens, especially for cooking small amounts of food.

The best guide to how your own oven works and how to get the most from it is the manufacturer's instruction booklet, which you should read and understand before you begin, and refer back to often. There are some basic rules to remember, though, and as in conventional cooking most are common sense:

Quantity

Food quantities affect cooking times. Generally, if you double the quantity of a recipe, you need to increase the cooking time by about half as much again.

Density and Shape

The denser the food, the longer the cooking time. When cooking foods of various densities or shapes at the same time, place the thicker part of the food to the outside of the dish, thinner part toward the middle. Arrange pieces of food in a circle whenever possible, and in a round dish. If neither of these arrangements is possible, cover the thinner or less dense part of the food with foil for part of the cooking time.

Size

The smaller a piece of food the quicker it will cook. Pieces of food of the same kind and size will cook at the same rate. Add smaller or faster-cooking foods further along in the cooking cycle. If you have a choice of cooking heights, put food that is larger and can take more heat above food that is smaller and more delicate.

Covering

Most foods will cook, reheat or defrost better when covered. Use special covers that come with your cookware, or simply cover with plastic wrap. This covering must be pierced to release steam, otherwise it can balloon and possibly burst. Tight coverings can give foods a "steamed" taste. Wax paper or paper towels can also be used to keep in the heat and increase cooking efficiency.

There has been some question as to the safety of plastic wrap for use in microwave ovens. When exposed to heat, some of the plasticisers used in the manufacture of these wraps can transfer into the food. At present, brands of plastic wrap are on the market which are made in a different way, avoiding the use of harmful plasticisers, and which thus circumvent the problem.

Standing Time

Microwave recipes usually advise leaving food to stand for 2-10 minutes after removal from the oven. Slightly undercooking the food allows the residual heat to finish it off, and microwave recipes take this into consideration. In general, foods benefit from being covered during standing time.

Using the Right Equipment

The number of different baking dishes and the range of equipment for microwave cooking is vast. Explore cookware

Facing page: infusing, that is heating liquids almost to boiling point with flavoring ingredients and leaving them to stand before straining, improves flavor.

Equipment

Type	Uses	Special Instructions
Browning Dish	Chops, steaks, sausages, stir-frying, nuts, eggs.	Pre-heat to instructions.
Ceramic	Pies, cakes, quiches, casseroles, vegetables, desserts.	Use plastic wrap if no covers. Cook and serve in same dishes.
China	Reheating.	Plate meals in advance. Avoid china with gold or silver trim. Use cups for tea. Reheat soup.
Cooking Bags	Frozen food, reheating, fish, vegetables.	Pierce bag to release steam cut across top to open after cooking.
Corning Ware	Casseroles, pies, quiches, vegetables, desserts.	See ceramics.
Custard Cups	Poach eggs, bake custards, small cakes.	Do not use metal or painted cups.
Glass Measures	Heat liquids. Make sauces.	Use a large enough size to allow stirring and whisking.
Glass Dishes, Casseroles	See ceramic.	See ceramic. Wine glasses for warming only. Thin glass may crack.
Metal	Combination ovens only.	Use insulating mat according to oven instructions.
Paper Plates, Cups, Containers	Breads, rolls, cakes, beverages, use for defrosting and reheating.	Absorb moisture. Best used on defrost or medium settings.
Paper Towels	Cooking bacon. Defrosting and reheating bread, rolls, cakes, covering defrosting foods.	Absorb moisture and fat. Remove immediately from the food after cooking.
Muffin Pans	Egg poaching. Small cakes, custards.	Line with paper cases for cakes.
Plastic	Various uses – casseroles, freezer to oven. Good for reheating and defrosting.	Remove lids from plastic boxes before heating. Not suitable for some combination ovens. Foam containers only suitable for warming. Fatty or sugary foods can cause melting.
Plastic Wrap	Covering dishes.	Pierce to release steam. Do not stretch too tightly. Lift carefully to avoid steam.
Pottery	Cooking and reheating.	Some painted or glazed finishes unsuitable. Avoid metal trim.
Pyrex	See glass.	
Straw Baskets, Bamboo Steamer	Warm rolls, reheat vegetables.	Use for serving. Use only for warming or reheating.
Tupperware	See plastic.	
Waxed Paper	Covering, lining baking sheets.	Prevents spattering. Holds in heat.
Wood	Warming bread rolls.	Can warp or dry out if heated too long.

departments and find your own favorites. Follow your oven instruction booklet carefully since it will give you good advice on which cookware is best for your particular oven. In general, microwave energy penetrates rounded shapes particularly efficiently, so round dishes, oval dishes and ring molds work very well.

Browning dishes do work, and the results are impressive. There are several different designs, but all are treated with a special material that absorbs microwaves and becomes extremely hot. You can seal the surface of meat just as you would in a frying pan and some dishes have lids, allowing you to stew or braise in the same dish. Use oven gloves or pot holders to remove browning dishes from the oven, and set them on a heat-proof mat to protect work surfaces. The equipment chart lists the most common items and their main uses.

These pages: various stages in caramel making.

Mention should be made of the use of foil in microwave cooking. Some manufacturers do not recommend its use, so you must consult your instruction booklet. If you can use it you will find it helps protect the breast bone of poultry, thin ends of roasting joints, heads and tails of whole fish, tender parts of vegetables, in fact any part of the food that is likely to cook too quickly.

There are a number of basic techniques that, once mastered, can make food preparation faster and easier, with better finished results:

Softening, Melting and Infusing

Butter, margarine and shortening are high in fat so they readily attract microwave energy and soften and melt quickly. To soften, heat on MEDIUM – MEDIUM LOW for 10-50 seconds for ½ cup.

Mix softened butter or margarine with an equal amount of flour to form a thickening paste for sauces – *beurre manie* in French, kneaded butter in English. This can be refrigerated or frozen in small amounts for use whenever you need a thickening agent.

Softened butter can be mixed with herbs, garlic, anchovy paste, tomato paste and cheese, to name but a few ingredients, and used on bread, baked potatoes, vegetables, fish, meat and poultry. Mix butter with honey, jam or fruit purées to spread on bread or scones.

Softened butter, margarine or shortening creams faster and more easily for baking mixtures. It will be easier to incorporate the sugar to get a light fluffy mixture and a lighter result after baking.

Melt butter, margarine or shortening more quickly, with less chance of burning small amounts. 1 tbsp takes just 30-40 seconds to melt on HIGH.

Clarified butter is much easier to make in a microwave oven than by conventional means. 1 cup melts in 1¼-2 minutes on HIGH. The salt in the butter will immediately

Above left: a selection of microwave baking dishes. Above: melting chocolate. Facing page: to dissolve gelatine, soak in liquid and melt until clear.

rise to the surface and can be skimmed off. Allow the butter to stand 2 minutes to let the milk solids settle to the bottom and then carefully spoon off the butter oil. Use on fish, vegetables, to seal a pâté or for conventional sautéeing.

Browned butter, the classic French *beurre noisette*, is easy to make in a microwave oven. Heat 1 cup butter on HIGH for 5-6 minutes, stirring twice. The butter will turn golden brown and have a nutty flavor. Enhance it with lemon juice or a sprinkling of herbs.

Cheese melts and softens rapidly in a microwave oven, but because it has a high protein content, it can toughen and become stringy. A MEDIUM setting is best to melt cheese sprinkled on as a topping. For this purpose, try Emmental, Gruyère, mozzarella or mild Cheddar. Very hard cheeses and mature Cheddar become crisp when melted and will look curdled in a sauce.

When making a cheese sauce, add finely grated cheese to the hot mixture and stir. Cover tightly and set aside. The cheese will melt smoothly in the residual heat. Stir once more and serve.

Facing page: softening cream cheese, butter and honey or jam makes for easier measuring and mixing. This page: softening hard brown sugar with a slice of apple in a loosely sealed plastic bag.

Cream cheese, curd cheese and ricotta often need to be softened before use. 6 tbsps of these cheeses will soften in 30-60 seconds on MEDIUM. Be sure to remove cream cheese from its foil wrapper and gently mash this type of cheese with a fork as it softens.

Cheese tastes best served at room temperature, but if you forget to take it out of the refrigerator there is an instant remedy. Heat hard cheese, such as Cheddar, on MEDIUM LOW for 30-45 seconds and soft cheese, such as Brie, for 15-30 seconds.

Syrups such as molasses, corn syrup and honey are easier to measure when liquefied for a minute or two on HIGH. Some syrups, like pure maple syrup, will crystallize slightly after opening unless used quickly, but when melted on HIGH for 1-2 minutes will become clear again. Certain varieties of honey are naturally thick and crystalline. 2-3 minutes on

HIGH is enough to make them clear and liquid. Stir all syrups and honey while they are melting to ensure even heat.

Soften hard brown sugar by sprinkling lightly with water and adding a slice of apple to the sugar in a plastic bag. Tie loosely and microwave on HIGH for 30-60 seconds. Leave to stand 5 minutes. Check after 15 seconds for amounts under 1 cup.

Chocolate should be melted on a MEDIUM setting and stirred often. High temperatures can cause chocolate to crystallize and harden. There is no need to add water to chocolate when melting it as there is no chance of scorching in a microwave oven.

Combine chocolate and margarine or shortening, ½ tsp fat for every ½ oz chocolate, to melt for drizzling, making dessert or liqueur cups or painting onto leaves to use as decoration. The chocolate will be more liquid when warm, but will still solidify when cool.

To make chocolate curls, soften block chocolate on LOW for 30-60 seconds or until just barely warm. Turn the block over halfway through the time. Draw a swivel vegetable peeler across the surface towards you to form curls. Use to decorate cakes and desserts.

To melt gelatine, sprinkle 1 tbsp onto no less than 3 tbsps liquid in a small dish. Leave to stand 2-5 minutes to soften. Microwave on HIGH for 1-2 minutes or until liquid and clear. If the gelatine in a dessert, such as a cold souffle, sets before you want it to, melt it again in the oven for 30-60 seconds.

Jams and jellies melt on HIGH in about 30 seconds for

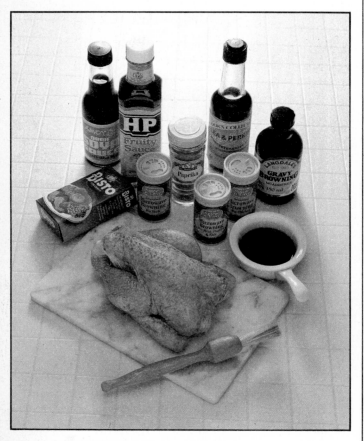

This page: a selection of browning agents that give appetizing color to meat and poultry. Facing page: toppings to give an appealing finish to baked goods.

2 tbsps. 1 cup will melt in 1½-2 minutes. Use as toppings for puddings, cakes or ice cream. Use as glazes for fruit tarts or even meat and poultry. Warm jam is also much easier to spread as a cake filling.

Soften peanut butter to make it easier to add to other ingredients for cake or biscuit recipes or simply to spread on bread.

Heat ice cream for about 30 seconds on MEDIUM to soften and make it easier to scoop to serve. To add flavorings to ice cream, scoop 4 cups into a large bowl and soften 30-60 seconds on MEDIUM, stirring well. Stir in toasted nuts, finely chopped chocolate, chopped fruit or liqueurs and

refreeze. Pack into decorative molds or even mixing bowls in several different layers to make bombes.

Sugar dissolves in water or other liquids easily without crystallizing. Double the quantity of liquid to sugar will make a simple syrup for poaching fruit. Equal measures of water and sugar cooked on HIGH for 10-12 minutes will caramelize. Do not allow the syrup to get too brown, though, as it continues to darken after it is removed from the oven.

Give cooking liquids more flavor by heating them nearly to the boiling point with flavoring ingredients and leaving them to infuse before straining to use.

For Bechamel sauce, use a slice of onion, a bay leaf, and a few black peppercorns in the milk.

Infuse whole coffee beans or vanilla pods in milk or cream for ice creams or mousses and custards.

Add citrus peel to liquids for poaching fish or for fruit and dessert sauces.

Browning, Basting and Topping

Use bastes or glazes that have soy sauce, Worcester sauce or gravy browning to give color to meat and poultry. The addition of marmalade, redcurrant jelly or honey to a glaze will help it cling to the food.

When using dry breadcrumbs or crushed cereals as a coating for meat, fish or poultry, dip or brush food with melted butter to help the coating stick. Toasted ground nuts also make a good coating for meat or poultry. Sprinkle the top of casseroles with breadcrumbs toasted in melted butter, crushed corn flakes or potato chips, grated cheese or simply paprika.

Add ingredients like nuts, cocoa, spices or herbs to pastry, or use whole-wheat flour.

Crushed cookies, bran, oatmeal, browned nuts, and streusel toppings are but a few ideas to give an appetizing appearance to microwave baked goods. Mix brown sugar and spices to sprinkle on as well. Colorful frostings or glazes are also an idea. There are also sprinkle-on microwave seasonings, which react with heat to give flavor as well as color to a whole range of foods.

Preserving and Pickling

Sterlilize jars the easy way. Add about 2 tbsps water to clean jars or bottles. Heat on HIGH for 2-3 minutes and drain upside-down on paper towels. Metal lids and rubber seals, however, are best sterilized outside the microwave oven. Paraffin wax for sealing is impervious to microwaves, and so must be melted conventionally.

Whole preserved fruit and pickled vegetables cannot be heated long enough to kill bacteria so they must be stored in the refrigerator.

Should pectin be necessary to help jams set, it can be added at the same time as other ingredients.

Prepare flavored vinegars and oils by sterilizing attractive bottles and adding herbs, spices, garlic, onions, fruit or citrus peel. Pour over a good quality vinegar or oil and heat briefly to help the flavors infuse. Store in a cool place.

Microwave preserving is cleaner, cooler and quicker than by the conventional method, and you will have no sticky pots to wash. You can also make preserves and pickles in smaller quantities for more variety.

This page: cook tender vegetables directly on their serving dishes. Facing page: very little liquid is needed to plump dried fruit.

Fruit and Vegetable Cookery

Vegetables cook quickly in the microwave, and with very little water, so they retain their color, texture and nutrients. Usually, 4-6 tbsps of water is all that is necessary for 1lb. Frozen vegetables usually don't need water.

Cover dishes when cooking vegetables and always snip two steam holes in the plastic wrap. Whole vegetables, such as cauliflower or corn-on-the-cob, can be wrapped

Cooking Vegetables

Type	Quantity	Mins. on High	Mins. Stdg. Time
Artichokes	4	10-20	5
Asparagus	1lb	9-12	5
Eggplant	2 med.	7-10	5
Beans	1lb		
Green		8	3
Lima		10	3
Beets	2	10-12	3
Whole			
Broccoli	1lb	6-10	3
Brussels Sprouts	1lb	7-9	3-5
Cabbage	1lb		
Shredded		7-9	3
Quartered		9-12	5
Carrots	8oz		
Whole		18	6
Sliced		10	5
Cauliflower	1lb		
Whole		11-13	3
Florets		7-10	3
Chicory	4	5	3
Corn-on-the-Cob	2 ears	6-8	3
Zucchini	1lb	5	3
Fennel	1 bulb		
Sliced		2-8	3
Quartered		10-12	
Leeks, sliced	1lb	10-12	3
Mushrooms	8oz	2	3
Okra	8oz	4	3
Onions, small	8oz	7-8	3
Sliced	2	10	3
Parsnips	8oz	8-10	3
Peas, shelled	1lb	10-15	5
Pea pods	8oz	2-3	3
Peppers	2 sliced	3	3
Potatoes			
New	1lb	10-12	5
Baked	2	9-12	5
Boiled	1lb	6-7	5
Spinach	8oz	4-5	3
Turnips	8oz	12	3

completely in plastic wrap and cooked with no water. Vegetables cooked in their skins, such as potatoes, need no covering, but skins should be pierced several times with a fork to release steam.

Cut vegetables to an even size, or choose those of nearly the same size so they cook in the same length of time. Arrange tender portions of vegetables, such as the tips of asparagus spears or flower ends of broccoli, to the center of the dish wherever possible, since the microwave oven will begin cooking at the outer edge of the dish first.

Facing page: rehydrating dried pulses in a microwave oven cuts out the need for overnight soaking. This page: for microwave "stir-frying" use a browning dish.

Rearrange large vegetables or turn them over halfway through cooking time. Stir cut vegetables occasionally to ensure even cooking.

To blanch vegetables for freezing, cook as usual, but put immediately into cold water to stop cooking. Drain and

spread on paper towels to dry completely. Pack in freezer containers or boiling bags. Alternatively, spread vegetables out on baking trays and freeze, uncovered. Once solid, pack and freeze. This will keep large vegetables in individual pieces and small vegetables free-flowing. You can even blanch vegetables inside the boiling bags. When cooked, chill in cold water, pat the bag dry and freeze in the same bag.

Peel peaches and apricots easily by bringing water to the boil – 4 cups takes about 8-10 minutes – and dropping in a

This page: heating citrus fruit in a microwave makes it possible to extract more juice. Facing page: "blanching" onions, nuts and tomatoes for easier peeling.

few pieces of fruit at a time. Leave to stand 1-2 minutes, depending on the ripeness of the fruit. Transfer to cold water. The peel should come off easily.

Peel tomatoes in the same way. Pickling or button onions can be cooked briefly in boiling water – about 1 minute. The

These pages: to defrost frozen foods, microwave in the serving dish and stir to break up lumps and distribute heat evenly.

However, both pasta and rice cook without sticking together and without the chance of overcooking. This is because most of the actual cooking is accomplished during

skins should come off easily, leaving the onions whole.

Get more juice from lemons, limes and oranges by heating 20-30 seconds on HIGH.

Slightly underripe avocados can be softened by the same method.

To plump up dried fruit, sprinkle with water and cover. Microwave on HIGH for 30-60 seconds, stirring occasionally. Leave to stand, covered, for 2-3 minutes. Substitute brandy or rum, lemon or orange juice for the water, if desired, and stir the fruit into ice creams, cake mixtures or sauces.

Eliminate overnight soaking for pulses with the microwave rehydrating method. Place dried peas, beans or lentils, covered with water, in a large bowl or casserole and cover tightly. Microwave for 8-10 minutes on HIGH, or until the water boils. Boil for 2 minutes more and leave to stand, covered, for 1 hour. Pulses will take almost as long to cook in a microwave oven as they do by conventional methods, but they do not become as starchy or mushy. Do make sure pulses are fully cooked; it is dangerous to eat them undercooked.

Rice and Pasta Cookery

Rice and pasta take nearly as long to cook in a microwave oven as they do on the stove top.

Cooking Rice and Pasta

Type	Quantity	Water	Mins. on High	Mins. Stdg. Time
Brown Rice	1 cup	2 cups	20	5
White Rice (long grain)	1 cup	2 cups	10-12	5
Quick Cooking Rice	1 cup	1½ cups	6	5
Macaroni	3 cups	3½ cups	6	10
Quick Cooking Macaroni	3 cups	3½ cups	3	10
Spaghetti	8oz	3½ cups	6-10	10
Tagliatelle/Fettucine	8oz	3½ cups	5-9	10
Pasta Shapes	3 cups	3½ cups	6	10
Lasagne Ravioli Cannelloni	6oz-8oz	3½ cups	6	10

standing time. All kinds of rice and shapes of pasta benefit from being put into hot water with a pinch of salt and 1 tsp oil in a deep bowl. There is no need to cover the bowl during cooking, but, during standing time, a covering of some sort will help retain heat. Soak large pieces of pasta, such as lasagne or long spaghetti, in hot water to soften before cooking. This will ensure that they remain completely submerged throughout the cooking time. Rinse all shapes of pasta thoroughly in hot water to remove most of the starch.

Reheating and Defrosting

Most ovens incorporate an automatic defrosting control in their setting programs. If your oven does not have this facility, use the lowest temperature setting and employ an on/off technique. Turn the oven on for 30 seconds-1 minute and then let the food stand for a minute or two before repeating the process. This procedure allows the food to defrost evenly without starting to cook at the edges.

Always cover the food when defrosting or reheating. Plastic containers, plastic bags and freezer-to-table ware can be used to freeze and defrost food in.

Meals can be placed on paper or plastic trays and frozen. Cover with plastic wrap or wax paper.

Usually, foods are better defrosted first and cooked or reheated second. There are exceptions to this rule so be sure to check instructions on pre-packaged foods before proceeding. Food frozen in blocks should be broken up as it defrosts. Use a fork to tear out small shreds of ground beef from the main block as it defrosts. Remove defrosted pieces and continue with the remainder. Carefully ease pieces of vegetable or fruit out as they defrost.

When reheating foods in a sauce, stir occasionally to distribute heat evenly. Spread food out in an even layer for uniform heating. To tell if reheating is completed, touch the bottom of the plate or container. If it feels hot, then the food is ready. Foods can be arranged on plates in advance and reheated very successfully, an advantage when entertaining.

Give foods new life when reheating. Add Worcestershire or soy sauce to stews and sauces.

Pasta and rice reheat superbly without overcooking. Use this to your advantage to create almost instant meals. Toss pre-cooked pasta or rice in butter and add herbs or garlic and cheese. Pre-cook onions, mushrooms, peppers or other vegetables and add with ham, shrimp or other pre-cooked meat or fish.

Personalize convenience foods by adding other ingredients such as tomato paste, wine, herbs and spices before reheating.

Make stock in your microwave oven and then freeze it for instant use anytime. Stock can be frozen in large blocks for soups, or in ice cube trays to add just a small amount to sauces.

Egg Cookery

In microwave ovens, the yolk of an egg, which contains more fat, cooks before the white. For this reason, standing time is very important as it allows the white to finish cooking without toughening the yolk.

Eggs can be fried in a browning dish. Preheat the dish according to the manufacturer's instructions and melt butter or margarine or fry bacon first and use some of the fat. Break in two eggs and they will fry in about 15-30 seconds, with 2-3 minutes standing time.

Scrambled eggs are even easier and they are much lighter and fluffier than those conventionally cooked. Butter isn't necessary except for flavor, so the calorie conscious can leave it out. Eggs will scramble in about 1½ minutes. They will begin to set around the edge of the dish first, so occasional stirring is necessary for even cooking. Standing time is important to allow the eggs to finish cooking in residual heat. Try additions such as chopped mushrooms, peppers or green onions in your scrambled eggs.

Make a soufflé or puffy omelet in a round pie dish in about 3-5 minutes on a MEDIUM setting. These omelets are

Defrosting

	Mins. on Low/ Defrost Setting per 1lb	Mins. Stdg. Time	Instructions
Pork, Veal, Lamb, Beef for Roasting	8-10	30-40	Pierce covering. Turn frequently.
Ground Beef or Lamb	7-8	5-6	Pierce wrapping. Break up as it defrosts.
Hamburgers	6-8	5	Use shorter time if individually wrapped. Pierce wrapper and separate when starting to defrost. Turn patties over once.
Bacon	6-8	5	Cover in paper towels. Separate as slices defrost.
Sausages	6-8	5	Cover in paper towels. Separate as defrosting.
Whole Chickens, Duck, Game Birds	5-7	30	Pierce wrapper. Remove giblets as soon as possible. Cover leg ends, wings, breast bone with foil part of the time. Turn several times.
Poultry Pieces	6-8	15-20	Pierce wrapper. Turn several times.
Casseroles, filled crêpes (for 4 people)	4-10	10	Defrost in dish, loosely covered. Stir casseroles if possible.

	Mins. on Low/ Defrost Setting per 1lb	Mins. Stdg. Time	Instructions
Vegetables	1-8	3-5	Cover loosely. Break up or stir occasionally.
Fish Fillets and Steaks	6-10	5-10	Pierce wrapper. Separate during defrosting. Use greater time for steaks.
Whole Fish	6-8	10	Pierce wrapper. Turn over during defrosting. Cover tail with foil halfway through.
Shellfish	6-8	6	Pierce wrapper. Stir or break up pieces during defrosting.
Bread Loaf	2-4 (per average loaf)	5-10	Cover with paper towels. Turn over once.
1 Slice Bread	20 seconds	1	Cover in paper towels.
Rolls 6 12	1½-3 2-4	3 5	Cover in paper towels. Turn over once.
Cake	1½-2	2	Place on serving plate. Some frostings not suitable.
Fruit Pie 9"	8-10	6	Use a glass dish. Place on inverted saucer or rack.

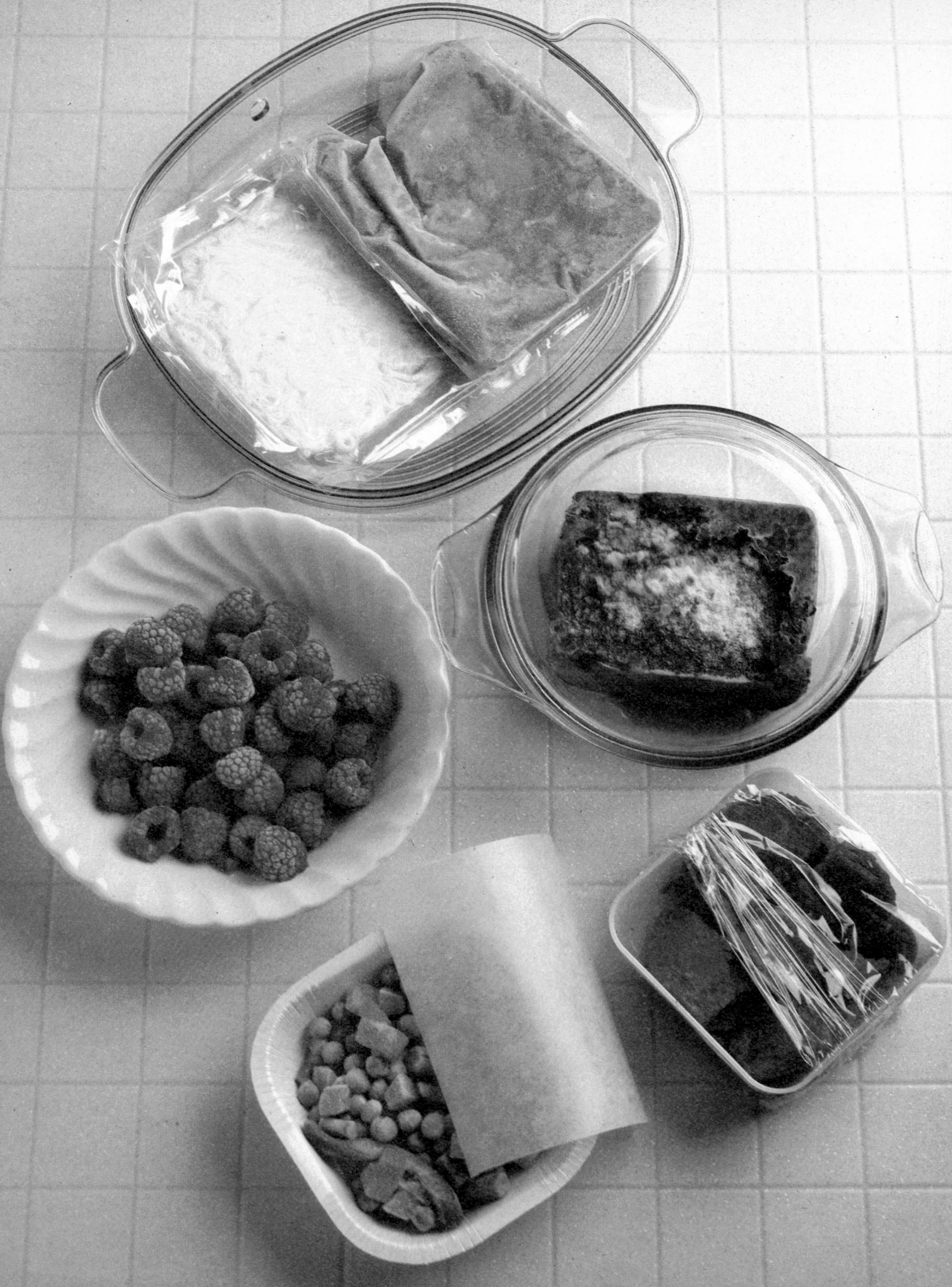

Reheating

	Quantity	Setting	Time from room temp. (minutes)	Special Instructions
Spaghetti Sauce	8oz 1lb	Med.	5-6 7-8	Stir several times. Keep loosely covered.
Beef Stew	8oz 1lb	Med.	5-5½ 6-7	Stir occasionally. Cover loosely.
Casseroles	8oz 1lb	Med.	5-7 7-8	Stir occasionally. Cover loosely. Use the shorter time for chicken, fish or vegetables.
Chili	8oz 1lb	Med.	5-5½ 6-7	Stir several times. Keep loosely covered.
Pork Chops	2 4	Med.	5 7½	Turn over halfway through. Cover loosely.
Lamb Chops	2 4	Med.	4-5 6-10	Turn over halfway through. Cover loosely.
Sliced beef, pork, veal	4oz 8oz	Med.	3-5 6-7½	Add gravy or sauce if possible. Cover loosley.
Sliced turkey, chicken, ham	4oz 8oz	Med.	2½-5 4-6	Add gravy or sauce if possible. Cover loosely.

	Quantity	Setting	Time from room temp. (minutes)	Special Instructions
Pasta	4oz 8oz	Med. or High	2-3 5-6	Stir once or twice. Add 1 tsp oil. Use shorter time for High setting.
Rice	4oz 8oz	Med. or High	2-3 4-5	Stir once or twice. Add 1 tsp oil or butter. Use shorter time for High setting.
Potatoes	4oz 8oz 1lb	High	1-2 2-3 3-4	Use the shorter time for mashed potatoes. Do not reheat fried potatoes. Cover loosely.
Corn-on-the-Cob	2 ears 4 ears	High	2-3 4-6	Wrap in plastic wrap.
Carrots	8oz 1lb	High	1-2 2-4	Cover loosely. Stir once.
Turnips	8oz 1lb	High	1-2 2-4	Cover loosely. Stir carefully.
Broccoli Asparagus	4oz 8oz	High	2 2	Cover loosely. Rearrange once.
Peas Beans Zucchini	4oz 8oz	High	1-1½ 1½-2	Cover loosely. Stir occasionally.

Facing page: a few of the many types of container that can be used for defrosting and reheating food in the microwave oven. Right: when poaching eggs, prick the yolk to prevent bursting.

versatile and can be filled with savory ingredients for a appetizer or light meal, or with jam or fruit for a dessert.

Beautifully-shaped poached eggs are easy in a microwave oven. Measure 2 tbsps of water in a custard cup and add ¼ tsp vinegar. Cover and bring to the boil. Break in an egg and pierce the yolk with a skewer to prevent bursting. Arrange cups in a circle on the turntable and cook on MEDIUM for 2-3 minutes for 4 eggs. Cover and leave to stand 2-3 minutes to finish cooking. If chopped hard-cooked eggs are needed, simply poach the eggs 1-2 minutes longer and chop after standing time. *Never* cook an egg in its shell; it will burst due to build up of steam.

To make egg-based sauces such as Hollandaise or custard sauce, use a deep bowl or glass measure to allow room for

Facing page and above left: stir scrambled eggs often during cooking time for a lighter, fluffier result. Allow standing time to finish cooking. Above: cover the thin ends of poultry joints with foil to prevent overcooking. Chicken breasts can be given color by "branding" with a hot skewer.

Meat and Poultry (per 1lb.)

	Mins. on High	Mins. on Medium	Internal Temperature Before Standing	After Standing
Beef: boned and rolled				
rare	6-7	11-13	130°F	140°F
medium	7-8	13-15	150°F	160°F
well-done	8-9	15-17	160°F	170°F
Beef: bone in				
rare	5	10	130°F	140°F
medium	6	11	150°F	160°F
well-done	8	15	160°F	170°F
Leg of Lamb	8-10	11-13	170°F	180°F
Pork	9-11	13-15	180°F	185°F
Ham				
Uncooked, boned	1st 5	15-18	130°F	160°F
Bone in	1st 5	15½-18½	130°F	160°F
Pre-cooked, boned	1st 5	12-15	130°F	
Bone in	1st 5	10-15		
Chicken	6-8	9-11	185°F	190°F
Duck	6-8	9-11	185°F	190°F
Turkey	9-11	12-15	185°F	190°F
Poussins	15-20 total			

whisking and keep a bowl of cold water on hand to dip the base of the cooking bowl in if the sauce starts to curdle. A Hollandaise sauce made with 2 egg yolks will cook in about 1 minute on MEDIUM. The sauce should be whisked every 15 seconds. A 2 egg yolk custard sauce cooks in about 1 minute on LOW if the yolks are added to a hot sauce. Flavor Hollandaise sauce with chopped herbs and a dash of tarragon vinegar to make Bernaise sauce – delicious on steak or fish. Liqueurs, chocolate or coffee make interesting additions to a basic custard sauce.

Meat and Poultry

The leanest and most tender cuts of meat available should be chosen for cooking in the microwave. Braising and stewing

Small Cuts of Meat, Poultry and Game

Type	Mins. on High	Mins. on Medium	Special Instructions
Steaks (1½" thick) 4-6oz			Use a browning dish pre-heated to manufacturer's instructions. Use timing for rare when cooking kebabs
rare	2-3		
medium rare	3-4		
medium	5-7		
well-done	7-9		
Lamb Chops	7-9		Use a browning dish
		13-15	Cook in liquid
Lamb Fillet		10-12	Brown, then cook in liquid
Pork Chops	7-9		Use a browning dish
		13-15	Cook in liquid
Pork Fillet		15	Brown, then cook in liquid
Veal Chops	7-9		Use a browning dish
		13-15	Cook in liquid
Smoked Pork Chops	4-6		Pre-cooked and browned
Ham Steaks	3		Pre-cooked and browned
Ground Meat (1lb)	5		Break up with a fork as it cooks
Hamburgers	2½-3		Use browning dish
Lamb Patties	2½-3		Use browning dish
Meatballs (1½ lbs)	10-12		
Duck Portions			Use browning dish
1 Breast (boned)	6		
2 Legs		15	Brown each side first
Chicken			
1 Breast		2-3	Brown first if desired
1 Leg		3-4	
2 Pieces		3-6	
3 Pieces		4-7	
4 Pieces		7-9	
Turkey Cutlets		10-15	
Turkey Legs (1lb)	1st 10	13-16	
Bacon		4	On rack or paper towels
		1	Per side on pre-heated browning dish
Sausages		2	Use browning dish

Use MEDIUM settings to cook most meats and whole birds. Hamburgers and smaller cuts of meat such as chops and steaks can be cooked on HIGH.

A browning dish is excellent for cooking these small cuts. They will require no standing time when cooked in this way. Use a browning dish for cubed meats for stews to give a little natural color to the sauce and to seal in the meat juices.

Meatballs can be cooked in a browning dish or arranged in a circle in a casserole and cooked with or without a sauce. Either way, they need to be rearranged several times during cooking.

Sausages must be cooked in a browning dish to give them color, but there is a choice of methods for bacon. Use a microwave roasting rack or place strips between paper towels to absorb fat as the bacon cooks. Prick the skins of sausages to prevent bursting.

Large joints of meat and poultry must be turned several times during cooking and should be covered during standing time.

Drain the drippings at intervals during cooking since this liquid will attract the microwave energy away from the meat or poultry and slow down cooking.

Foil is very effective in protecting the thinner parts of joints and birds. Remove the foil about halfway through cooking time.

Variety meats, such as liver or kidneys should be pricked with a fork several times to prevent bursting.

Fish and Seafood

A fillet of fish cooks in 2-3 minutes, while shellfish take even less time. Cooking should end when the fish or seafood is slightly undercooked so that standing time can finish it off without toughening and drying out.

Arrange fillets in a circle with the thinner ends toward the center of the dish. Cover with paper towels or add liquid and cover with plastic wrap. The liquid can be water and lemon juice or wine, and the addition of a bay leaf, onion slice and a few black peppercorns gives a good flavor. This liquid can then be used to make a sauce for the fish.

To keep the thin ends of salmon or cod steaks in place, secure with wooden picks. Turn steaks over halfway through cooking time.

Whole fish can be "fried" in a browning dish. They can also be poached in bags, shallow, covered dishes or enclosed in wax paper – en papillote. To keep the head or tail of a large, whole fish such as salmon from over-cooking, wrap it in foil. Be sure to check the instruction booklet of your particular oven, though, before using foil. Wrap the foil in several layers of plastic wrap and cover the body with a single layer, if desired. If the fish is too large for your dishes, or will not lie flat on the turntable, curve it to fit and loop string loosely

steak can be used, but there will be no real time saving as these cuts need slow cooking to tenderize them. However, the more expensive cuts will not shrink as much, so they are more economical to use.

Facing page: a whole small fish can be "fried" in a browning dish.

Fish and Shellfish (per 1lb.)

Type	Mins. on high	Type	Mins. on high
Cod Steaks and Fillets	4-5	Salmon (Whole) per 1lb	8-9
Halibut and Turbot Steaks and Fillets	4-5	Salmon Steaks and Tail pieces	2-7
Smoked Fish (poached)	1-2	Sea Bass (Whole) per 1lb	8-9
Sole Fillets	2-3	Shrimp Langoustines	2-5
Mackerel	10-12	Scallops	2-5
Trout	8-10	Mussels	2-3
Herring Fillets	6-8	Oysters	1-2
Tuna Steaks	5	Squid	6
Monkfish Tail Portion Sliced	8-9 2-5		

Above: cook fish "en papillote", in parchment or in cooking bags, to keep in moisture and flavor. Wrapping foil around the head and tail of a fish (top far right) will help protect these parts from overcooking, while cling film wrapped around the fish (right) protects the skin and retains the heat. Far right: curve a large fish to fit the oven turntable.

around the head and tail to keep the fish in shape. Make sure that the foil ends do not touch the sides of the oven as the fish turns. Remove foil halfway through cooking time.

Shellfish can toughen if cooked too quickly at too high a temperature. Add them to a hot sauce and leave to stand 5 minutes to cook in residual heat. Alternatively, cook small pieces of shellfish for about 3 minutes on HIGH, or use a lower setting for a slightly longer time. The following chart is a quick guide to cooking times for fish and shellfish but, as with all cooking, the results will vary from oven to oven.

Open oysters by heating them 45 seconds on HIGH. They will prise open much more easily.

Baking

Baking is one of the most surprising things a microwave oven does. Quick breads, those leavened with baking powder or soda and sour milk, rise higher than they do in a conventional oven and they bake more quickly. If using a square or loaf dish, cover the corners with foil for part of the cooking time to keep that part of the bread or cake from drying out before the middle is cooked. Cakes also rise much higher and a single layer will bake in about 6 minutes on a medium setting.

The dough-like microwave meringue mixture (facing page top) will triple in size once cooked (facing page bottom). Above: baking a pastry shell on an inverted saucer allows the base to crisp.

Eliminate salt from cake batters as it tends to make the batter bubble, causing a very coarse texture.

Microwave ovens can cut the rising time for yeast doughs nearly in half, and a loaf of bread will bake in an astonishing 8-10 minutes.

Cookies will not usually crisp in a microwave oven. However, they bake to a moist, chewy texture which is often just as pleasing. A batch of 3 dozen will cook in about 10 minutes, one batch at a time.

Pastry is not as much of a problem as most people believe. Prick the base and sides of the pastry well after lining a pie or flan dish. It is essential to bake the pastry shell "blind" – without filling – in order to dry the base. Pastry will not bake to an even brown, but it will crisp. Alternatives are sweet or savory cookie or cracker crusts.

To let air and heat circulate underneath breads, cakes and

pastry shells, place them on a rack or inverted saucer. This allows the base to cook faster and more evenly. Once baked and cool, keep microwave-baked goods well covered. They seem to dry out faster than those conventionally baked.

Microwave meringues are the real magic trick. The mixture is prepared like thick frosting and must be pliable enough to shape. Cut very small pieces of the mixture and place well apart on a microwave baking sheet; the meringues will triple in size and become light and crisp. The amount of powdered sugar needed will vary with the size and age of the egg white. New eggs tend to have more liquid whites which take up more sugar. Soft meringues for topping pies will rise beautifully but will not brown. Sprinkle lightly with brown sugar or toasted coconut, or broil for a few seconds.

Above: warming the liquid helps dissolve yeast. Top right: foil wrapped around the corners of a rectangular baking dish ensures even cooking. Right: a decorative ring mold for microwave cakes. Facing page: poppadums microwave to perfect crispness if first brushed with a little oil.

Special Tips

Here are several microwave "secrets" that don't seem to fall into any particular category:

* Dry herbs for storage by placing sprigs between paper towels and microwaving until the herbs can be crumbled. Cool and seal tightly.

* Heat grated citrus peel from 1 orange or 2 lemons on a plate for 1-2 minutes on HIGH. Leave to cool completely until dry and store in airtight containers.

* To skin almonds, bring 1 cup water to the boil in about 2-3 minutes on HIGH and add 1 cup nuts. Microwave 1 minute on HIGH and drain. The skins should slip off easily.

* For chestnuts, make a horizontal cut in the rounded side and place in a bowl of water. Cover and bring to the boil. Boil 1 minute on HIGH and leave to stand 5-10 minutes. Peel one chestnut at a time, leaving the others covered in water.

Microwaving is the ideal way of drying herbs (above), citrus peel and crumb toppings (facing page).

* Nuts such as pecans, walnuts or Brazils should be brought to the boil in water in a covered bowl. Leave to stand 1 minute, drain and cool. Open carefully; the shells will fill with water. The nuts should come out whole.

* Toast nuts, sesame seeds and sunflower seeds in melted butter for 3-7 minutes for nuts and 3-4 minutes for seeds on HIGH. Stir often while microwaving, and do not allow them to brown too much. They will darken as they cool.

✻ Coconut needs no fat to toast. Sprinkle in an even layer on a plate and heat on MEDIUM for 3-4 minutes, tossing frequently with a fork. Leave to cool and store in airtight containers.

✻ Crisp cereals and snack foods on paper towels for 15-60 seconds on HIGH. Allow to cool.

✻ Wrap bread, rolls or coffee cake in paper towels and heat 15-30 seconds on HIGH to warm and freshen.

✻ To make croûtons, cut bread into ½ inch cubes and spread in an even layer on a baking dish. Microwave 4-5 minutes on HIGH, stirring every 2 minutes until dry. Leave to cool and store airtight or freeze. For flavored croûtons toss in melted butter and sprinkle with herbs, garlic powder or grated Parmesan cheese before microwaving.

✻ Cut bread in cubes and microwave 4-5 minutes on HIGH. Cool and crush in a blender or food processor to make breadcrumbs for toppings and coatings. Store in airtight containers or freeze.

Facing page: the warm, even temperature required for yogurt-making is easily maintained in a microwave oven. Above left: a few moments in the microwave ensure that cereals and snack foods can be served perfectly crisp. Above: croûtons made the microwave way. Left: when warming bread or freshening a slightly stale loaf, wrap in paper towels to absorb moisture.

* Warm brandy 15 seconds on HIGH for drinking, 30 seconds on HIGH in a heatproof container for flaming. Ignite with a match OUTSIDE the oven.

* To make yogurt, pour 3½ cups milk into a large bowl. Heat on HIGH until the temperature reaches 190°F. Stir several times while heating. Cool the mixture to 115°F and stir in ⅓ cup natural yogurt. Cover the bowl and reheat on MEDIUM-LOW when the temperature falls below 115°F. Allow to stand 3-4 hours. Check the temperature frequently and reheat as before, at least every 30 minutes. Refrigerate when the mixture sets, and keep no longer than 2 weeks.

* Cook poppadums by brushing both sides lightly with oil and cooking 30 seconds on HIGH for one. Wontons can be cooked in the same manner.

* Popcorn needs special equipment. *Do not* try to pop it in a paper bag. It will often catch fire!

*Make your own liqueurs using brandy or vodka as a base. Add colorings and flavorings of your choice to a sugar syrup and heat about 5 minutes.

*Specialty coffee- and tea-based drinks are easy to make and take about 5 minutes heating. A warming cup of hot chocolate takes about 2 minutes.

Recipe Conversion

Once you master the art of microwave cooking, the time will come when you want to adapt your favorite recipes. To convert your own recipes, follow these rules:

*Look for similar microwave recipes with the same quantities of solid ingredients, dish size, techniques and times.

Whether toasting nuts and coconut (this page) or making a cup of tea or coffee (facing page), the microwave oven will perform it perfectly.

*Reduce liquid quantities by one quarter. More can always be added later in cooking.

*Fat will attract microwave energy and slow down the cooking of the other ingredients in the recipe. Cut the amount used by at least half.

*Reduce the seasoning in your recipe; microwave cooking intensifies flavors.

*Microwave cooking takes approximately a quarter of the time of conventional cooking. Allow at least 5 minutes standing time before checking to see if the food is cooked. You can always add a bit more time at this point if necessary.

Microwave
THE RECIPES

The second part of this book is devoted to recipes using the knowledge and techniques you have gained from the first part. The more you apply them, the more you will enjoy your microwave oven.

SOUPS AND APPETIZERS

Stuffed Avocados

PREPARATION TIME: 10 minutes

MICROWAVE COOKING TIME:
10 minutes

SERVES: 4 people

½ cup milk
2 black peppercorns
1 small bay leaf
1 slice onion
1 small blade mace
1½ tbsps butter or margarine
2 tbsps flour

FILLING
2 tomatoes, skinned, seeded and chopped
3oz cooked, peeled shrimp
½ cup mushrooms, roughly chopped
4 green onions, roughly chopped
1 tbsp chopped parsley
1 tsp chopped marjoram
Dash tabasco
Salt and pepper
2 avocados, halved and stoned
Juice of half a lemon

TOPPING
⅓ cup grated Parmesan cheese
4 tbsps dried breadcrumbs

Pour the milk into a large glass measure and add the bay leaf, peppercorns, blade mace and a slice of onion. Heat on HIGH for 2 minutes and then leave to stand for 5 minutes, loosely covered. Melt the butter or margarine in a small, deep bowl for 30 seconds on HIGH. Stir in the flour and when well mixed strain on the infused milk. Heat for 2 minutes on HIGH until thickened, stirring frequently. Add the tomatoes, shrimp, mushrooms and green onions to the sauce. Add the parsley, marjoram and dash of tabasco and season with salt and pepper. Scoop the flesh out of the avocado, leaving a ¼ inch lining inside each shell. Sprinkle the scooped out flesh and shell with lemon juice. Stir the flesh

This page: Stuffed Avocados (top) and Oeufs en Cocotte (bottom). Facing page: Crab and Tomato Quiche (top) and Country Pâté (bottom).

into the other ingredients in the sauce and spoon the sauce into the avocado shells. Combine the Parmesan cheese and breadcrumbs and sprinkle over the top of each avocado. Cook the avocados for 3 minutes on HIGH, or until the sauce is bubbling slightly. Brown under a broiler if desired and serve immediately. NOTE: this recipe may be prepared with slightly under-ripe avocados, which will soften in the microwave oven.

Tomato Chartreuse

PREPARATION TIME: 15 minutes plus chilling time

MICROWAVE COOKING TIME: 4½-8 minutes

SERVES: 4 people

*Juice of half a lemon made up to ½ cup
    with cold water*
1 tbsp gelatine
1½ cups tomato juice
½ tsp tomato paste
1 bay leaf
Salt and pepper

GARNISH
3oz mushrooms, sliced
3 green onions, chopped
3 tbsps olive or vegetable oil
1 tbsp white wine vinegar
Salt and pepper
Chopped mixed herbs

Combine the lemon juice and water in a small glass bowl and sprinkle over the gelatine. Allow to soak for 5 minutes. Combine the tomato juice, tomato paste, salt, pepper and bay leaf in a large glass measure or bowl. Microwave the tomato mixture on HIGH for 2½-5 minutes or until boiling. Allow to stand for 2 minutes and remove the bay leaf. Heat the gelatine mixture for 1-2 minutes on HIGH and pour into the tomato mixture when the gelatine dissolves. Dampen a 2½ cup mold and pour in the tomato mixture. Alternatively, use 4 individual molds. Chill in the refrigerator until set, about 2 hours. To speed up the setting process put into the freezer for 30 minutes, remove and place in the refrigerator until set. Combine the mushrooms and the olive oil in a small bowl and cook for 1 minute on HIGH, stirring occasionally. Leave to cool and combine with the vinegar, green onions and salt and pepper. Add a pinch of chopped mixed herbs and set aside. When the tomato mixture has set, loosen from the sides of the mold and turn out onto a serving plate. Alternatively, dip the mold into warm water for 30 seconds to help loosen the mixture. Pile the mushroom mixture on top of the mold or each individual mold using a draining spoon to drain away excess dressing. Serve chilled.

Oeufs en Cocotte

PREPARATION TIME: 10 minutes

MICROWAVE COOKING TIME: 9 minutes

SERVES: 4 people

1 tbsp butter or margarine
4oz mushrooms, chopped
2 tbsps flour
4 tbsps dry white wine
2 tbsps milk
2 tsps chopped mixed herbs
1 tbsp capers, chopped
4 eggs
Salt and pepper
4 tbsps heavy cream
Paprika
Nutmeg

Place the butter in a small casserole and melt on HIGH for 30 seconds. Add the chopped mushrooms and cook for 2 minutes on HIGH. Stir in the flour and add the wine and milk. Cook for a further 1-2 minutes on HIGH, or until thickened. Add the capers, mixed herbs and salt and pepper to taste. Divide the mixture into 4 custard cups and make a well in the center of the mixture in each

Right: Tomato Chartreuse.

dish. Break an egg into the center of the mixture in each cup. Pierce the yolk once with a sharp knife. Cook for 3-4 minutes on HIGH or until the white is set and yolk is still soft. Place a spoonful of cream on top of each egg and sprinkle with paprika and nutmeg. Cook for 1 minute on LOW to heat the cream. Serve immediately.

Crab and Tomato Quiche

PREPARATION TIME: 20 minutes

MICROWAVE COOKING TIME: 18 minutes plus 6 minutes standing time

SERVES: 4 people

PASTRY
1 cup whole-wheat flour
4 tbsps margarine
2 tbsps vegetable shortening or lard
Pinch salt
4 tbsps ice cold water
3 eggs
4 tbsps light cream
Salt and pepper
½ cup shredded cheese
½ cup frozen peas
2 green onions, finely chopped
6oz white crabmeat or crab sticks, flaked
4 tomatoes, peeled and sliced

TOPPING
1 tbsp dry, seasoned breadcrumbs
2 tbsps grated Parmesan cheese

Put the flour, salt, margarine and shortening into the bowl of a food processor and work until the mixture resembles fine breadcrumbs. With the machine running, add the water gradually until the dough holds together. It may not be necessary to add all the water. Roll out the pastry on a floured board to ⅛ inch thickness and place in an 7 inch pie dish. Trim the edge and flute the pastry. Refrigerate for 10 minutes. Beat the eggs with the salt, pepper and the cream. Add the cheese, peas, onions and crabmeat. Prick the base of the pastry and cook it on HIGH for 2-3 minutes, or until starting to

crisp. To help crisp the base, place the pastry on an inverted saucer or a microwave oven rack. Pour the filling into the pastry shell and decorate the top with the tomatoes. Cook on MEDIUM for 10 minutes. Mix the topping ingredients together and sprinkle over the top of the quiche 5 minutes before the end of cooking. Serve hot or cold.

Curried Chicken Kebabs with Cucumber Sauce

PREPARATION TIME: 10 minutes

MICROWAVE COOKING TIME: 6 minutes

SERVES: 4 people

3 chicken breasts, skinned and boned

MARINADE
2 tbsps vegetable oil
1 clove garlic, crushed
2 tsps curry powder
¼ tsp cayenne pepper
1 tbsp chopped coriander leaves
Juice and grated rind of 1 lime
Salt and pepper

SAUCE
½ cucumber, grated
1 cup plain yogurt
1 tbsp chopped fresh mint
1 tsp mango chutney
Pinch salt and pepper

Cut the chicken into 1 inch wide strips. Combine the ingredients for the marinade and mix in the chicken to coat each piece. Leave to marinate for 1 hour. Thread the chicken onto wooden skewers and put onto a microwave roasting rack. Cook for 5 minutes on HIGH, turning the kebabs frequently while cooking. Leave to stand, covered, for 1 minute. While the chicken is marinating,

Right: Curried Chicken Kebabs with Cucumber Sauce.

sprinkle the grated cucumber lightly with salt and leave to stand. Rinse thoroughly and pat dry with paper towels. Combine with the remaining sauce ingredients and serve with the chicken kebabs.

Country Pâté

PREPARATION TIME: 10 minutes

MICROWAVE COOKING TIME: 15 minutes

SERVES: 6-8 people

8oz ground pork
8oz ground veal
4oz ham, ground
4oz pork liver
3oz ground pork fat
1 clove garlic, crushed
4 tbsps brandy
Ground allspice
Thyme
1 bay leaf
2 tsps green peppercorns
8 slices bacon, bones and rind removed
Salt and pepper

Place the ground pork, veal and ham in a food processor. Remove the skin and ducts from the liver and add to the meat in the food processor. Add the pork fat, garlic, brandy, allspice, thyme and salt and pepper. Process once or twice to mix thoroughly, but do not over-mix. The mixture should be fairly coarse. Stir in the green peppercorns by hand. Line a glass loaf dish with the bacon and press the meat mixture into the dish on top of it. Place the bay leaf on top of the mixture, fold any overlapping edges of the bacon over the top and cover the dish with a double layer of plastic wrap. Place the dish of pâté in a larger shallow dish with hot water to come halfway up the sides of the pâté dish. Cook on MEDIUM for 6 minutes. Leave to stand for 5 minutes, then cook a further 10 minutes on MEDIUM. Cover with foil, press down and weight. Leave to chill 2-4 hours or overnight. Remove bay leaf and cut mixture into thin slices to serve.

Watercress and Potato Soup

PREPARATION TIME: 10 minutes

MICROWAVE COOKING TIME: 20 minutes

SERVES: 4 people

3 tbsps butter or margarine
1 shallot, finely chopped
1lb potatoes, peeled and diced
1½ cups chicken or vegetable stock
Salt and pepper
1½ cups light cream
1 bunch watercress
Ground mace
Dash lemon juice

Put the butter, shallot and potatoes into a large bowl. Loosely cover and cook for about 2 minutes on HIGH. Add the stock, salt and pepper and re-cover the bowl. Cook for about 15 minutes or until the vegetables are soft. Reserve 4 small sprigs of watercress for garnish and chop the remainder, removing any thick stems. Add the chopped leaves to the other ingredients in the bowl, re-cover and cook for another 2 minutes on HIGH. Allow the soup to cool for a few minutes and pour into a food processor. Purée until smooth. The soup should be lightly flecked with green watercress. Return the soup to the bowl and add the cream. Cook for 3-4 minutes on LOW or MEDIUM until heated through. Do not allow the soup to boil. Stir in a pinch of ground mace and lemon juice to taste. Serve the soup garnished with small sprigs of watercress. May be served hot or cold.

Stilton and Walnut Soup

PREPARATION TIME: 10 minutes

MICROWAVE COOKING TIME: 18 minutes

SERVES: 4 people

3 tbsps butter or margarine
1 large onion, finely chopped
4 tbsps flour
1½ cups chicken stock
1 bay leaf
1 sprig thyme
Salt and pepper
1½ cups milk
2 cups Stilton cheese, crumbled (half Cheddar and half blue cheese may be substituted)
4 tbsps heavy cream
4 tbsps chopped walnuts

Put the butter and the onion into a large bowl and loosely cover with plastic wrap, pierced several times. Cook for 6 minutes on HIGH, stirring occasionally. Stir in the flour, add the stock gradually and mix well. Add the bay leaf, thyme and salt and pepper and cook, uncovered, for 10 minutes on HIGH. Remove the herbs and crumble the cheese into the soup. Add the milk and stir to mix well. Cook for 1 minute on HIGH, uncovered. Stir in the cream and cook a further 1 minute on HIGH. Serve garnished with the chopped walnuts.

Facing page: Stilton and Walnut Soup (top) and Watercress and Potato Soup (bottom).

Microwave

100 MICROWAVE SECRETS

FISH AND SEAFOOD

Herring Lyonnaise

PREPARATION TIME: 20 minutes

MICROWAVE COOKING TIME:
13-14 minutes

SERVES: 4 people

4 even-sized herrings, gutted, fins trimmed
  and heads removed, if desired
Seasoned flour for dredging
4 tbsps butter or margarine
2 large onions, peeled and thinly sliced
1 red pepper, seeded and thinly sliced

Cut 2 slits in the skin on the side of
each herring and set them aside. Heat
a browning dish according to the
manufacturer's directions and when
hot drop in half the butter. Cook the
onions and peppers for 4-5 minutes
on HIGH to brown slightly and
soften. Set aside and reheat the
browning dish. Meanwhile, dredge
the herring in flour and when the
browning dish is hot, drop in the
remaining butter. Cook the herring
2 at a time for 2 minutes per side on
HIGH. Repeat with the remaining
herring. Place all the herring in a
serving dish and top with the onions
and the peppers. Reheat for 1 minute
on HIGH and serve immediately.

Seafood Kebabs

PREPARATION TIME: 20 minutes

MICROWAVE COOKING TIME:
6-7 minutes plus standing time

SERVES: 4 people

8oz jumbo shrimp
8oz monkfish tails
1 green pepper, seeded and cut into 2 inch
  pieces

1 red pepper, seeded and cut into 2 inch
  pieces
8 even-sized mushrooms, stems trimmed

BASTING MIXTURE
2 tbsps soy sauce
1 tsp coarsely ground black pepper

**This page: Cod with Crispy
Topping (top) and Seafood Kebabs
(bottom). Facing page: Herring
Lyonnaise (top) and Sardines with
Mustard and Herbs (bottom).**

½ tsp grated fresh ginger
1 tsp lemon juice
½ tsp honey

Peel the shrimp and cut the monkfish tails into an equal number of 1 inch cubes. Thread onto 4 wooden skewers, alternating with the remaining ingredients. Mix together the basting ingredients and brush over the kebabs. Place on a microwave-proof roasting rack in a shallow dish and cook on MEDIUM for 6-7 minutes, turning and basting frequently until the fish is cooked and the shrimp have turned pink. Allow to stand, covered, for 1-2 minutes before serving. If any basting mixture remains after cooking, pour over the kebabs to serve.

Sweet and Sour Shrimp

PREPARATION TIME: 20 minutes
MICROWAVE COOKING TIME:
7-10 minutes
SERVES: 4 people

SAUCE
1½ tbsps cornstarch mixed with 4 tbsps
    water
½ cup light brown sugar
8oz can unsweetened pineapple pieces
1 green pepper, seeded and sliced
1 clove garlic, crushed
6 tbsps white wine or cider vinegar
1½ tbsps soy sauce
2 tbsps tomato ketchup
2 tomatoes, peeled and quartered
3 green onions, diagonally sliced
Salt and pepper
1lb cooked, peeled shrimp

Mix the cornstarch and water in a large glass measure or deep bowl and mix in the sugar. Drain the pineapple and add the juice to the bowl. Add the pepper, garlic, vinegar, soy sauce, tomato ketchup and salt and pepper. Cook, uncovered, for 5-7 minutes, stirring after 1 minute, until the sauce clears and thickens. Add the reserved pineapple and the tomatoes and green onions to the sauce. Leave the sauce to stand, covered, for 5 minutes. Stir in the shrimp and heat

on MEDIUM for 2-3 minutes until all the ingredients are hot. Serve with rice or crisp chow mein noodles.

Cod with Crispy Topping

PREPARATION TIME: 10 minutes
MICROWAVE COOKING TIME:
9-11 minutes
SERVES: 4 people

TOPPING
4 tbsps butter or margarine
1½ cups seasoned breadcrumbs
2 tbsps paprika
4 tbsps grated Parmesan cheese
2 tbsps sesame seeds
2 tsps chopped parsley
Salt and pepper

FISH AND POACHING LIQUID
4 cod fillets
Juice of 1 lemon
½ cup water
1 bay leaf
4 black peppercorns

GARNISH
Lemon wedges

Heat a browning dish according to the manufacturer's directions. Melt the butter or margarine in the dish and add the breadcrumbs. Stir well and heat for 1 minute on HIGH until lightly brown. Add the remaining ingredients and heat for a further 1 minute on HIGH. Set aside. Put the cod, lemon juice, water, bay leaf and peppercorns into a casserole. Cover loosely with plastic wrap or waxed paper and cook for 5-6 minutes on HIGH. Allow the fillets to stand for 1-2 minutes and then lift out of the poaching liquid with a draining spoon. Place the fish on a serving plate and top each fillet with some of the breadcrumb mixture. Heat through for 30 seconds-1 minute on HIGH and serve with lemon wedges.

Right: Sweet and Sour Shrimp.

Trout en Papillote

PREPARATION TIME: 20 minutes

MICROWAVE COOKING TIME:
23 minutes plus standing time

SERVES: 4 people

4 10oz trout, gutted and trimmed
2 carrots, peeled and cut into matchsticks
3 sticks celery, cut into matchsticks
2 small leeks, trimmed, washed and
  shredded
4 tbsps butter
4 tbsps white wine
2 tsps thyme
2 tsps chopped parsley
Salt and pepper
4 small bay leaves

Place each fish on a sheet of lightly-oiled waxed paper. Place the carrots in a small casserole with 2 tbsps water, cover and cook on HIGH for 2 minutes. Add the celery and cook a further 2 minutes on HIGH. Add the leeks and continue cooking for 1 minute on HIGH. Add salt and pepper. Place an equal portion of the vegetables on top of each trout. Melt the butter for 30 seconds on HIGH and put 1 spoonful on top of each trout along with 1 spoonful of white wine. Place 1 bay leaf on top of each trout and seal the parcel. Cook on HIGH for 9 minutes per 2 fish parcel. Repeat with the remaining 2 fish and allow to stand for 3 minutes before opening to serve.

Sardines with Mustard and Herbs

PREPARATION TIME: 25 minutes

MICROWAVE COOKING TIME:
9 minutes

SERVES: 4 people as a main course or 6 as an appetizer

12-16 sardines, depending upon size
1 tbsp olive oil
1 shallot, finely chopped
4 tbsps whole grain mustard
2 tbsps dry white wine
2 tbsps chopped fresh mixed herbs
Salt and pepper

GARNISH
Lemon or lime wedges
Parsley sprigs

Cut the sardines, rinse well and pat dry. Place head to tail in a large, shallow dish. Heat the oil in a small bowl for 30 seconds on HIGH and

**This page: Trout en Papillote.
Facing page: Whole Poached
Salmon.**

add the chopped shallot. Cook for 2 minutes on HIGH to soften the shallot. Stir in the mustard, white wine, chopped herbs and salt and

pepper. Loosely cover the sardines with plastic wrap or waxed paper, and cook on HIGH for 3 minutes. Turn the sardines over and spread with the mustard and herb mixture. Cook, uncovered, for 4 minutes on HIGH, or until the fish is cooked. Brown under a preheated broiler, if desired, before serving. May be served as an appetizer or as a main course with new potatoes and a green salad.

Whole Poached Salmon

PREPARATION TIME: 20 minutes
MICROWAVE COOKING TIME: 8-9 minutes per 1lb
SERVES: 6-8 people

3½ lb salmon, cleaned, with head and tail left on
Whole fresh herbs, such as dill or tarragon
Oil for brushing

GARNISH
Lemon slices or wedges
Sliced cucumber
Fresh herbs

Wash the salmon and pat dry. Place fresh herbs inside the cavity of the fish and brush the skin on both sides with oil. Use foil to cover the thin end of the tail and the head to prevent overcooking. Cover the foil with several thicknesses of plastic wrap. Make an incision along the skin on either side of the dorsal fin to allow steam to escape so that the skin does not burst. Lay the fish flat on the turntable, if it will fit, or curve it to fit the shape of the turntable. If curving the fish, tie loosely with string to hold the shape. Cook 8-9 minutes per 1lb on LOW or DEFROST. About halfway through the cooking time, uncover the head and tail and remove the string to allow the head and tail to cook through. To test the salmon to see if it is cooked, slip a sharp knife through one of the slits made on either side of the dorsal fin. If the blade passes through without resistance, the fish is cooked. Allow

the fish to cool slightly and then peel away the skin carefully. Start at the dorsal fin with a sharp knife and carry on peeling with a round-bladed table knife which should slip easily between the skin and the flesh. Carefully transfer the fish to a serving plate, removing the herbs inside the cavity. Garnish with cucumber, lemon slices or wedges and fresh herbs to serve. Serve hot with new potatoes and hollandaise sauce or cold with mayonnaise and a green salad.

Oysters à la Crème

PREPARATION TIME: 15 minutes
MICROWAVE COOKING TIME: 5 minutes
SERVES: 4 people

2 dozen oysters on the half shell or unopened
4 tbsps heavy cream
4 tbsps cream cheese
1 tbsp chopped parsley
Salt and pepper
Nutmeg

GARNISH
Coriander leaves

Scrub the oyster shells well, if unopened, and leave to soak in clean water for 2 hours. Arrange in a circle on the microwave turntable and cook on HIGH for 45 seconds-2 minutes. After 45 seconds insert a short-bladed knife near the hinge and prise open. If the oysters do not open easily, they need further cooking for up to 2 minutes. Remove any pieces of broken shell from the inside and place oysters in a circle on the turntable. Mix together the heavy cream, cream cheese, parsley and salt and pepper. Top each oyster with some of the cheese mixture. Sprinkle with nutmeg and heat through 2-3 minutes on MEDIUM. Garnish with coriander and serve immediately.

Right: Oysters à la Crème.

MEAT AND POULTRY

Poulet en Cocotte

PREPARATION TIME: 20 minutes

MICROWAVE COOKING TIME:
35-45 minutes

SERVES: 4-6 people

12-14 small onions
2 tbsps butter or margarine
1 clove garlic, crushed
2 tbsps flour
10oz canned beef consommé
½ cup dry white wine
12 small new potatoes, peeled
1 sprig fresh rosemary
1 sprig fresh marjoram or thyme
Salt and freshly ground black pepper
3lbs chicken
4oz mushrooms, left whole if small,
*   quartered if large*

Heat 2 cups water in a large bowl on HIGH until boiling. Drop in the onions and leave to stand for 2 minutes. Drain the onions, peel and trim the root ends. Melt the butter in a large casserole for 30 seconds on HIGH. Add the garlic and stir in the flour. Gradually pour on the consommé and white wine, stirring until well blended. Remove the leaves from the rosemary and the marjoram and add with salt and pepper. Truss the chicken legs, tuck the wing tips under and place the chicken in the casserole, spooning over the liquid. Place the new potatoes around the chicken and cover the dish tightly. Microwave on HIGH for 20-30 minutes, or until the meat in the thickest part of the thigh is no longer pink and the juices run clear. Baste the chicken frequently while cooking and stir the sauce to keep it smooth. Halfway through the cooking time add the peeled onions

and re-cover the dish. In the last 5 minutes of cooking, add the mushrooms. Remove the chicken from the cooking liquid and cut into 8 pieces. Return the chicken pieces to the casserole and spoon over the sauce to serve. Alternatively, serve chicken whole, coated with sauce and surrounded by vegetables.

Kidneys Turbigo

PREPARATION TIME: 15 minutes

MICROWAVE COOKING TIME:
20 minutes

SERVES: 4 people

1 tbsp oil
8oz small pork sausages, skins pricked all
*   over*
12 lambs' kidneys, halved and cored
8oz button onions, peeled
4oz small mushrooms, left whole
1 cup beef stock
1 tbsp tomato paste
2 tbsps sherry
1 bay leaf
¼ tsp thyme
2 tbsps cornstarch dissolved in 4 tbsps
*   cold water*
1 tbsp chopped parsley
Salt and pepper

Heat a browning dish according to the manufacturer's directions, add the oil and heat for 30 seconds on HIGH. Add the sausages and cook on HIGH for about 5 minutes, turning over several times during cooking, until lightly browned. Remove the sausages from the browning dish to a casserole. Reheat the dish and brown the onions

lightly. Add the onions to the sausages in the casserole along with the kidneys and mushrooms. Pour over stock and stir in the tomato paste. Add the sherry, bay leaf, thyme and salt and pepper and cover the dish. Cook on HIGH for 12 minutes, stirring frequently. Add the cornstarch and water mixture to the casserole and stir very well. Cook, uncovered, about 3 minutes or until the sauce thickens. Stir frequently after 1 minute. Remove the bay leaf before serving, and garnish with chopped parsley.

Roast Fillet of Beef with Herbs

PREPARATION TIME: 15 minutes plus marinating time

MICROWAVE COOKING TIME:
8-11 minutes plus standing time

SERVES: 6 people

½ cup red wine
2 tbsps red wine vinegar
3 tbsps oil
1 tsp each chopped tarragon, thyme,
*   rosemary and parsley*
2 tbsps Worcestershire sauce
1lb beef tenderloin

GARNISH
Fresh herbs

Combine all the ingredients for the marinade in a small, deep bowl and cook on HIGH for 2-3 minutes.

Facing page: Roast Fillet of Beef with Herbs (top) and Kidneys Turbigo (bottom).

Allow to cool completely. Place the beef in a plastic bag or a shallow dish. Pour over the marinade and turn the beef several times to coat thoroughly. If using a bag, tie securely and place on a plate or a dish. Chill for at least 4 hours, turning the meat several times. When ready to cook, place the beef on a microwave-proof roasting rack, tucking the thinner portion of the meat under slightly on the end. If desired, tie the meat at 1 inch intervals to help keep its shape. Cover 1-2 inches of each end of the beef with foil. Cook on HIGH for about 3 minutes and remove the foil from the beef. Lower the setting to MEDIUM and cook for 5-8 minutes longer, turning the beef over once. The internal temperature of the meat

This page: Poulet en Cocotte. Facing page: Duck with Peaches (top) and Lemon Pepper Chicken (bottom).

should register 130°F. Leave the meat to stand for 3 minutes before carving. Slice the meat thinly and surround with the fresh herbs to serve.

Lemon Pepper Chicken

PREPARATION TIME: 20 minutes

MICROWAVE COOKING TIME: 10 minutes

SERVES: 4 people

4 chicken breasts
Juice of 1 lemon
1 tbsp coarsely ground black pepper
Paprika
Salt

GARNISH
Lemon wedges
Watercress

Heat 4 metal skewers in a gas flame or on an electric burner. Skin the chicken breasts. When the skewers are red hot, make a criss-cross pattern on the chicken flesh with the hot skewers. It may be necessary to reheat the skewers after using once or twice. Place the chicken in a large casserole with the thinner end of the chicken breasts pointing towards the center. Sprinkle over the paprika, pepper, lemon juice and salt. Cover the dish tightly and cook 10 minutes on MEDIUM. It may be necessary to cook a further 5 minutes on MEDIUM if the chicken is not done. Baste occasionally with the juices during cooking. To serve, pour the pan juices back over the chicken and garnish with lemon slices and watercress.

Crispy Chicken

PREPARATION TIME: 15 minutes

MICROWAVE COOKING TIME: 9-12 minutes

SERVES: 4-6 people

3½ lbs chicken pieces

CRISPY COATING
1 cup crushed cornflakes
6 tbsps grated Parmesan cheese
½ tsp dry mustard
1 tsp paprika
½ tsp celery salt
½ tsp oregano
½ tsp parsley
Pepper

DIPPING MIXTURE
½ cup butter or margarine
2 eggs, beaten

Skin all the chicken pieces and remove any fat. Combine all the crispy coating ingredients and spread out evenly on a sheet of waxed paper. Melt the butter for 1 minute on HIGH and stir into the beaten eggs in a shallow dish. Dip the chicken into the egg and butter mixture or use a basting brush to coat each piece. Put the chicken pieces in the crumb mixture and lift the ends of the paper to help toss and coat the chicken. Place half the chicken in a glass dish, bone side down. Make sure the thickest pieces of the chicken are on the outside of the dish to start. Cover loosely with waxed paper. Cook on HIGH for 9-12 minutes. Rearrange and turn the chicken over halfway through the cooking time, and remove the paper. Keep the cooked chicken warm while cooking the remaining chicken. If necessary, cover the turntable with paper towels to reheat all of the chicken at once for 1-2 minutes.

Barbecued Spare Ribs

PREPARATION TIME: 15 minutes plus marinating time

MICROWAVE COOKING TIME: 20 minutes

SERVES: 4 people

MARINADE
3 tbsps Worcestershire sauce
1 tbsp soy sauce
3 tbsps tomato ketchup
1 tbsp honey
Gravy browning (optional)
3½ lbs pork spare ribs, cut into 1 rib pieces

Dissolve the marinade ingredients in a bowl and cook on HIGH for 1 minute. Leave to cool completely. Add the ribs to the marinade and stir to mix well. Cover and refrigerate for several hours, stirring the ribs occasionally. Transfer the ribs to a shallow dish or place in a microwave roasting dish. Cover with plastic wrap, pierced several times, and cook on HIGH for 10 minutes. Baste well with the marinade and turn the ribs over. Cook for a further 10 minutes on HIGH or until the ribs are tender. Serve with any remaining sauce.

Duck with Peaches

PREPARATION TIME: 20 minutes

MICROWAVE COOKING TIME: 18 minutes

SERVES: 4 people

4 breasts of duck, boned
4 tbsps butter or margarine
Salt and pepper
½ cup whole blanched almonds
1 tbsp cornstarch
1lb canned sliced peaches, drained and juice reserved
½ cup red wine
1 tbsp lemon or lime juice
1 bay leaf
Pinch cinnamon
Pinch nutmeg
2 tsps whole allspice berries

Heat a browning dish according to the manufacturer's directions. When hot, add the butter or margarine and allow to melt. Sprinkle both sides of each duck breast with salt and pepper. Place skin side down on the browning dish and press down well. Cook on the skin side for 6 minutes on HIGH. Turn the duck breasts over and cook a further 6 minutes on the other side. Remove the duck breasts to a covered casserole to stand while preparing the sauce. To brown the almonds for the sauce, reheat the browning dish briefly, add the almonds and heat for 1-2 minutes on HIGH, stirring occasionally until the almonds are a light golden brown. Mix the cornstarch with the peach juice, red wine, lemon juice, spices and bay leaf in a small, deep bowl or glass measure. Cook on HIGH for 6-7 minutes, stirring after 1 minute.

Facing page: Barbecued Spare Ribs (top) and Crispy Chicken (bottom).

Stir occasionally until thickened. Remove the bay leaf and add the browned almonds and the peaches to the sauce. Leave covered while finishing the duck. Cut each duck breast into thin slices and arrange on 4 serving plates. Spoon the peach sauce over the duck breasts to serve.

Tarragon Steak

PREPARATION TIME: 15 minutes

MICROWAVE COOKING TIME: 6 minutes for the sauce, as indicated in method for steak

SERVES: 4 people

4 fillet steaks, cut 1½ inches thick, brushed with oil on both sides
Salt
Freshly ground pepper
12 mushroom caps, fluted if desired

SAUCE
½ cup heavy cream
4 sprigs fresh tarragon
1 tsp Dijon mustard
Salt and pepper

First prepare the sauce. Pour the cream into a deep bowl or a glass measure. Remove the leaves from the sprigs of tarragon and leave whole or chop and combine with the cream. Cook the cream on HIGH for 6 minutes, until boiling and reduced and thickened. Stir in the mustard and the salt and pepper and leave covered while preparing the steaks. Heat a browning dish according to the manufacturer's directions. Sprinkle the steaks with salt and pepper and cook for 2 minutes on one side and 2½ minutes on the other for rare. For medium-rare, 2 minutes on one side and 3½ minutes on the other. For medium, 3 minutes on one side and 4½ minutes on the other. For well-done, 3 minutes on one side and 6 minutes on the other. Add the mushrooms at the same time as the steaks are cooking. For well-done steaks, remove the mushrooms halfway through cooking time. Remove the steaks and mushrooms to a serving plate and

keep warm. Pour the sauce into the browning dish and mix in the meat juices. Pour the sauce over the steaks to serve.

Marmalade Duckling

PREPARATION TIME: 15 minutes

MICROWAVE COOKING TIME: 40 minutes

SERVES: 3-4 people

4½-5lbs duckling
1 slice orange
1 slice onion
1 bay leaf
Salt

GLAZE
4 tbsps bitter orange marmalade, thin cut
4 tbsps soy sauce
½ cup chicken stock
2 tsps-1 tbsp cornstarch
Salt and pepper

GARNISH
Orange slices
Watercress

Place the slice of orange, slice of onion and bay leaf inside the duck cavity. Sprinkle the inside lightly with salt and pepper. Prick the duck skin all over with a fork and use some of the soy sauce from the glaze to brush on all sides of the duck. Sprinkle lightly with salt and place the duck breast side down on a microwave-proof roasting rack. Cook for 10 minutes on HIGH and drain well. Return the duck to the oven, reduce the power to MEDIUM and continue cooking for a further 15 minutes. Combine the remaining soy sauce with the orange marmalade. Turn the duck breast side up and brush with the glaze. Continue cooking for 15 minutes on MEDIUM, draining away the fat often and brushing with the glaze. Remove the duck from the roasting rack and leave to stand, loosely covered with foil, for 5 minutes before carving. Drain all the fat from the roasting dish but leave the pan juices. Combine the cornstarch,

chicken stock, salt and pepper and remaining glaze with the pan juices and pour into a small, deep bowl. Cook 2-3 minutes on HIGH until thickened. Remove the orange, onion and bay leaf from the cavity of the duck and put in a bouquet of watercress. Surround the duck with orange slices and spoon over some of the sauce. Serve the rest of the sauce separately.

Hamburgers

PREPARATION TIME: 15 minutes

MICROWAVE COOKING TIME: As indicated in method

SERVES: 4 people

1lb ground beef
1 small onion, finely chopped
4 tbsps Worcestershire sauce or soy sauce
Salt and pepper
4 hamburger buns
Lettuce and tomato (optional)

Combine the meat, onions, salt and pepper and mix well. Hamburgers may be cooked on a plate or roasting rack or in a pre-heated browning dish. If using the browning dish method, add the Worcestershire or soy sauce to the hamburger mixture. Shape into 4 even-sized patties. Pre-heat the browning dish according to the manufacturer's directions. For medium-rare hamburgers cook for 2 minutes on HIGH on the first side and 1-2 minutes on HIGH on the second side. For well-done hamburgers, cook 2½ minutes on the first side and 2-3 minutes on the second. Standing time is not needed for hamburgers cooked in a browning dish. To cook hamburgers on a plate or roasting rack, shape into patties and brush with the Worcestershire or

Facing page: Hamburgers (top) and Tarragon Steak (bottom).

This page: **Marmalade Duckling.**

soy sauce on both sides. Arrange the hamburgers on a roasting rack or on a plate lined with paper towels. Cover the hamburgers with waxed paper to prevent spatters. Use the same cooking times and setting as for hamburgers cooked on the browning dish, but allow the hamburgers to stand for 1-2 minutes before serving.

Microwave
100 MICROWAVE SECRETS

REHEATING AND DEFROSTING

Beef and Vegetable Stew

PREPARATION TIME: 20 minutes

MICROWAVE COOKING TIME:
29 minutes

SERVES: 4 people

2 tbsps oil
1lb frying or rump steak
2 tbsps flour
1 clove garlic, crushed
½ cup red wine
1 cup beef stock
Bouquet garni (1 sprig thyme, 1 bay leaf,
    3 parsley stalks)
Salt and pepper
1 tsp tomato paste
2 large carrots, peeled and cut into
    matchsticks
3 sticks celery, cut into matchsticks
3 small onions, quartered
4oz mushrooms, quartered

Heat a browning dish according to
the manufacturer's directions.
Meanwhile, trim the meat and cut
into 1 inch pieces. Pour the oil into
the browning dish and quickly brown
the meat on all sides. Pour the meat
juices and oil into a casserole dish
and mix in the flour. Add the garlic
and gradually stir in the wine and
stock. Add the bouquet garni, cover
the dish and cook on HIGH for 6
minutes, stirring every 2 minutes
until thickened. Add the meat to the
dish and re-cover. Cook on HIGH
for a further 15 minutes or until the
meat is tender. Adjust the seasoning
and leave the casserole to stand,
covered. Meanwhile, place the carrot,
celery and onion in a small bowl with
4 tbsps water. Cover and cook on
HIGH for 4 minutes. Add the
mushrooms and re-cover the dish.
Cook a further 4 minutes on HIGH

or until the vegetables are tender.
Remove the bouquet garni from the
meat and drain the vegetables. If
freezing, allow both the meat and
vegetables to cool completely and
freeze them in separate containers. To
defrost, heat the meat for 6-8
minutes on DEFROST or LOW,
breaking up the chunks of meat as
they defrost. Allow to stand 10-20
minutes before reheating. Defrost the
vegetables on LOW or DEFROST
for 4 minutes then leave to stand
before reheating. To reheat, combine
the vegetables and the meat in a
serving dish and cover well. Cook on
HIGH for 12-15 minutes until heated
through. If refrigerating, combine the
meat and the vegetables in a
casserole or serving dish and cover.
To reheat, cook on HIGH for 12-15
minutes or until heated through.
Serve the stew with rice, pasta or
potatoes.

Salade de Legumes

PREPARATION TIME: 15 minutes

MICROWAVE COOKING TIME:
2-4 minutes

SERVES: 6 people

9-10oz frozen or canned artichoke hearts
1 red onion, chopped or 4 green onions,
    thinly sliced
1 clove garlic, minced
1 green pepper, seeded and chopped
1 tsp chopped fresh basil
1 tsp chopped fresh thyme
2 tsps chopped parsley
1lb canned navy beans, rinsed and
    drained or white kidney beans or butter
    beans
4 tomatoes, peeled, seeded and chopped

DRESSING
3 tbsps olive oil
2 tbsps white wine vinegar
½ tsp Dijon mustard
Pinch salt and pepper

GARNISH
1 head radicchio
Few leaves curly endive

If using frozen artichoke hearts, place
in a large casserole dish and cover.
Microwave on HIGH for 3-4
minutes, or until slightly warm. Stir
in the remaining ingredients, except
the dressing and garnish, and cook
for 2 minutes on HIGH to warm
through. Mix the dressing ingredients
and pour over the warm salad and
toss to coat. Serve warm. Cover and
chill for at least 2 hours before
serving. Arrange the radicchio and
endive leaves on serving plates and
pile on the salad. Spoon over any
excess dressing to serve.

Convenient Vegetable Casserole

PREPARATION TIME: 5 minutes

MICROWAVE COOKING TIME:
15 minutes

SERVES: 4 people

2 cans mushroom soup or 1 can
    condensed soup with an equal measure
    of water
2 tbsps cornstarch dissolved in 4 tbsps
    heavy cream
9-10oz frozen mixed vegetables
Pinch ground nutmeg
1 tbsp chopped parsley

TOPPING
1 package crisp fried onions

Mix the soup with the cornstarch and heavy cream. Cook, uncovered, on HIGH for 6-7 minutes, stirring occasionally after 1 minute until thickened. Break up the mixed vegetables to separate and add frozen to the sauce. Add the nutmeg and parsley and stir well. Pour into a casserole or serving dish and microwave on HIGH for 5-8 minutes or until heated through. Sprinkle on the crisp fried onions and heat 30 seconds on HIGH. Serve immediately.

Vegetable Stock

PREPARATION TIME: 15 minutes

MICROWAVE COOKING TIME:
15 minutes

MAKES: 4 cups

8oz carrots, roughly chopped
6 sticks celery, roughly chopped
1 turnip, roughly chopped (optional)
3 onions, chopped and the peel of one reserved for color
1 tomato, quartered and seeded
3 parsley stalks
1 whole clove
1 bay leaf
1 blade mace
2 sprigs thyme or other fresh herbs
6 black peppercorns
Pinch salt
4 cups water

FOR CHICKEN STOCK
Add 8oz chicken pieces (if including giblets, discard chicken livers)

FOR BEEF STOCK
Add 8oz shin of beef, cut into small cubes and browned for 8 minutes in a preheated browning dish

FOR FISH STOCK
Add skin, bones and trimmings from 8oz fish

Combine all the ingredients for the required stock in a large bowl. Half-cover the bowl with plastic wrap and cook on HIGH for 15 minutes. The

stock will boil, so the bowl must be deep enough to contain it. Allow to stand for 15-20 minutes before straining. The stock will keep up to 3 days in the refrigerator. Alternatively, freeze the stock in ice cube trays for convenience. If the beef stock is not brown enough for your liking, a few drops of gravy browning can be added to the finished stock. Use the stock for soups and to prepare sauces and gravies.

Chicken Cacciatore

PREPARATION TIME: 20 minutes

MICROWAVE COOKING TIME:
35-45 minutes

SERVES: 4 people

3¼ lbs chicken, cut into 8 pieces and skinned
3 tbsps oil
1 medium onion, finely sliced
1 clove garlic, crushed
1 green pepper, seeded and thinly sliced
1 tbsp chopped fresh basil or 1½ tsps dried basil
1 bay leaf
Pinch ground nutmeg
4 tbsps red wine
6 tbsps chicken stock
8oz canned tomatoes, broken up
Salt and pepper
1 tbsp cornstarch mixed with 2 tbsps cold water
Grated Parmesan cheese (optional)

Place the oil and the onion in a large casserole dish and cook on HIGH for 3 minutes. Add the garlic, pepper, bay leaf, basil and nutmeg and a pinch of salt and pepper. Cover and cook on HIGH for 2 minutes. Pour in the wine, stock and tomatoes and stir well. Add the chicken and cook on MEDIUM for 30-40 minutes. About 6-7 minutes before the end of the cooking time, blend the cornstarch and the water and add to the

Right: Salade de Legumes (top) and Convenient Vegetable Casserole (bottom).

chicken, stirring in well. Cook until the sauce thickens. Allow to stand for 5 minutes before serving. To freeze, allow the chicken to cool completely and transfer to a serving dish or a freezer container. Cover well and store for up to 1 month. To thaw and reheat, microwave, uncovered, on HIGH for 15-20 minutes, stirring frequently. Sprinkle over grated Parmesan cheese, if desired, and serve with pasta or rice.

This page: Vegetable Stock. Facing page: Chicken Cacciatore (top) and Beef and Vegetable Stew (bottom).

EGG DISHES

Poached Eggs Hollandaise

PREPARATION TIME: 20 minutes

MICROWAVE COOKING TIME:
11-12 minutes

SERVES: 4 people

*1lb fresh spinach, stems removed and
  leaves well washed*
4 eggs

HOLLANDAISE SAUCE
1 stick butter
2 tbsps lemon juice
Pinch cayenne pepper
2 egg yolks
Salt and pepper
Paprika or nutmeg

Place the spinach in a roasting bag and secure loosely with string. Cook on HIGH for 5 minutes and drain very well, squeezing out excess moisture. Set aside while poaching the eggs. Pour 6 tbsps of hot water into each custard cup and add a drop of vinegar to each. Bring the water to the boil on HIGH for about 1½-2 minutes. Break an egg into each dish and pierce the yolk with a sharp knife or skewer. Arrange the dishes in a circle on the oven turntable and cook on HIGH for 2½-3 minutes or on MEDIUM for 3-3½ minutes. Give the dishes a half turn halfway through the cooking time. Loosen the eggs from the side of the dish with a knife and slip onto a draining spoon. Chop the spinach roughly and arrange in one large serving dish or four individual serving dishes and place an egg on top. Cover the dishes and keep warm while preparing the sauce. Place the butter for the sauce in a large glass measure or small, deep bowl and heat on HIGH for

1½ minutes. Mix the lemon juice with the cayenne pepper and egg yolks and whisk gradually into the hot butter. Cook on MEDIUM for 1 minute, whisking halfway through the cooking time. Make sure the sauce does not boil. If the sauce appears to be curdling, remove from the oven and dip the bowl or measure into cold water to stop the cooking. Whisk well and return to the oven for a further 1 minute or until thickened. Reheat the eggs and the spinach for 20 seconds on HIGH and pour over the sauce. Sprinkle either paprika or grated nutmeg on top of the sauce to serve.

Scrambled Eggs and Shrimp

PREPARATION TIME: 15 minutes

MICROWAVE COOKING TIME:
5-7½ minutes plus standing time

SERVES: 4 people

4 eggs
4 tsps butter or margarine
4 tbsps milk or light cream
1 tbsp chopped chives
2oz cooked, peeled shrimp
4 large ripe tomatoes
Salt and pepper

Place the butter in a glass measure or a small, deep bowl and cook on HIGH for about 30 seconds-1 minute. Beat the eggs with the milk and add a pinch of salt and pepper. Pour into the melted butter and cook on HIGH for 3-4½ minutes. Stir frequently while cooking to bring the set pieces of egg from the outside of the bowl to the center. When just

beginning to set, remove the eggs from the oven and stir in the chives and the shrimp. Allow to stand for 1-2 minutes to finish cooking. Meanwhile, cut the tomatoes into quarters or eighths but do not cut all the way through the base. Arrange the tomatoes in a circle on the turntable and heat through for 1-2 minutes on HIGH. To serve, press the tomatoes open slightly and fill each with some of the egg and shrimp mixture.

Asparagus and Tomato Omelet

PREPARATION TIME: 15 minutes

MICROWAVE COOKING TIME:
15 minutes

SERVES: 2 people

4oz chopped asparagus, fresh or frozen
2 tbsps water
6 tbsps milk
1 tsp flour
Salt and pepper
2 tomatoes, peeled, seeded and chopped
3 tbsps grated cheese
Paprika

Put the asparagus and water into a large casserole. Cover and cook for 5-6 minutes on HIGH. Leave to stand while preparing the omelet. Beat the egg yolks, milk, flour and salt and pepper together. Beat the egg whites until stiff but not dry and fold

Facing page: Poached Eggs Hollandaise (top) and Scrambled Eggs and Shrimp (bottom).

into the egg yolks. Melt the butter in a 9 inch glass pie dish for 30 seconds on HIGH. Pour the omelet mixture into the dish and cook on MEDIUM for 7 minutes or until softly set. Lift the edges of the omelet as it cooks to allow the uncooked mixture to spread evenly. Sprinkle with the cheese and spread on the drained asparagus and the chopped tomato. Fold over and cook for 1 minute on LOW to melt the cheese. Sprinkle with paprika and serve immediately.

Basic Custard Sauce

PREPARATION TIME: 5 minutes

MICROWAVE COOKING TIME: 3-4 minutes

MAKES: Approximately 1 cup

1 cup milk
1 vanilla pod
2 tbsps sugar
2 tsps cornstarch
2 egg yolks

Heat the milk and the vanilla pod for 2 minutes on HIGH and leave to stand for 10 minutes. Remove the vanilla pod from the milk. Mix together the sugar and the cornstarch in a small, deep bowl or a glass measure. Pour on the milk gradually, stirring constantly. Cook on HIGH for 3 minutes, stirring once or twice until the sauce thickens. Beat the egg yolks with 2 tbsps of the hot sauce, then pour into the bowl or measure and cook on LOW for 1 minute. Do not allow the sauce to boil or it will curdle. Cover with plastic wrap until ready to serve and then pour into a serving dish.

This page: Basic Custard Sauce. Facing page: Asparagus and Tomato Omelet.

VEGETABLES AND FRUIT

Stuffed Eggplants

PREPARATION TIME: 20 minutes

MICROWAVE COOKING TIME: 18-25 minutes

SERVES: 4 people

2 eggplants
1 tbsp butter or margarine
1 clove garlic, crushed
1 onion, finely chopped
1 small green pepper, seeded and chopped
2oz mushrooms, roughly chopped
2 cups canned tomatoes, chopped and
    juice reserved
1 tbsp tomato paste
2 tsps chopped basil
Pinch sugar
Salt and pepper

TOPPING
1 cup grated mozzarella cheese
1 tbsp dry breadcrumbs

Cut the eggplants in half lengthwise and score the flesh lightly. Sprinkle with salt and leave to stand for 20 minutes. Rinse well and pat dry. Wrap each eggplant completely in plastic wrap and cook on HIGH for 7-9 minutes. Leave to stand while preparing the filling. Melt the butter for 30 seconds on HIGH and add the garlic and onion. Cook for 1-2 minutes on HIGH and add the green pepper and mushrooms. Cook a further 2-3 minutes on HIGH and stir in the drained tomatoes and the tomato paste. Add the basil, sugar, salt and pepper and cover the bowl. Cook 6-8 minutes and set aside. Unwrap the eggplants and scoop out the flesh, leaving a ¼ inch lining inside the skin of each. Cut the flesh roughly and add to the tomato mixture. If the mixture looks dry, add some of the reserved tomato juice. Fill each eggplant shell and cook for 3 minutes on HIGH. Top with the mozzarella cheese and sprinkle each lightly with the breadcrumbs. Heat a further 2-3 minutes on LOW to melt the cheese before serving.

Dahl

PREPARATION TIME: 25 minutes

MICROWAVE COOKING TIME: 45 minutes plus 5-10 minutes standing time

SERVES: 4 people

8oz lentils, brown or green
4 tbsps butter or margarine
1 large onion, finely chopped
1 clove garlic, crushed
1 red or green chili pepper, finely chopped
1 tsp cumin
1 tsp coriander
1 tsp turmeric
½ tsp cinnamon
½ tsp nutmeg
3 cups vegetable stock
Salt and pepper
1 bay leaf
Chopped coriander leaves

ACCOMPANIMENT
4-8 poppadoms

Cover the lentils with water and soak overnight. Alternatively, microwave 10 minutes to boil the water and then allow the lentils to boil for 2 minutes. Leave to stand, covered, for 1 hour. Melt the butter or margarine for 1 minute on HIGH in a large casserole. Add the onion, garlic, chili pepper and spices. Cook 4 minutes on MEDIUM. Drain the lentils and add to the casserole with the vegetable stock. Cover and cook on HIGH for 45 minutes, or until the lentils are soft and tender. Allow to stand, covered, 5-10 minutes before serving. If desired, purée before serving and add the chopped coriander. To prepare the poppadoms, brush each side lightly with a little oil and cook one at a time on HIGH for about 30 seconds, or until crisp. To cook two together, microwave for 1½-2 minutes.

Red Bean Pilaf

PREPARATION TIME: 20 minutes

MICROWAVE COOKING TIME: 1 hour 23 minutes plus standing time

SERVES: 4 people

1 cup red kidney beans
1½ cups long-grain rice
2 tbsps butter or margarine
1 green pepper, diced
4 green onions, chopped
2 tbsps chopped parsley
2 tbsps desiccated coconut
Cayenne pepper
Ground nutmeg
Salt and pepper

Cover the beans with water and leave to soak overnight. Alternatively, microwave 10 minutes to boil the water, allow the beans to boil for 2 minutes and leave to stand 1 hour, covered. Drain and cover

Facing page: Red Bean Pilaff (top) and Dahl (bottom).

with fresh water and add a pinch of salt. Cook on MEDIUM for 55 minutes-1 hour. Allow to stand for 10 minutes before draining. The beans must be completely cooked. Save the cooking liquid to use as stock in other recipes if desired. Place rice in a large bowl or casserole dish and add 2 cups water and a pinch of salt. Cook for 10 minutes. Leave to stand for 5 minutes before draining. Heat the butter or margarine for 30 seconds on HIGH and add the pepper dice. Cook for 1 minute, stirring once or twice. Stir in the cayenne pepper, nutmeg, salt, pepper, rice and beans. Cook on HIGH for 1 minute. Add the green onions, parsley and desiccated coconut and cook a further 30 seconds on HIGH before serving.

Vegetable Stir-Fry

PREPARATION TIME: 20 minutes

MICROWAVE COOKING TIME: 7½ minutes

SERVES: 4 people

2 tbsps oil
4 spears broccoli
4oz pea pods, trimmed
4oz miniature corn
1 red pepper, seeded and sliced
½ cup water chestnuts, sliced
4oz mushrooms, sliced
1 clove garlic, minced
1 tbsp cornstarch
6 tbsps vegetable stock
4 tbsps soy sauce
2 tbsps sherry
4oz bean sprouts
2 green onions, sliced

Pre-heat a browning dish according to manufacturer's directions. Add the oil to the dish when hot. Cut off the broccoli flowerets and reserve them. Slice the stalks diagonally. Slice the miniature corn in half lengthwise. Put the sliced broccoli stalks and the corn together in the hot oil for 1 minute on HIGH. Add the red pepper, pea pods, water chestnuts, garlic, mushrooms and the broccoli flowerets and cook a further 1 minute on HIGH. Mix together the

cornstarch, vegetable stock, soy sauce and sherry in a glass measure or a small glass bowl and cook for 4 minutes on HIGH, stirring after 1 minute until thickened. Transfer the vegetables to a serving dish and pour over the sauce. Add the bean sprouts, green onions and cook a further 1 minute on HIGH. Serve immediately.

Cauliflower Mornay

PREPARATION TIME: 20 minutes

MICROWAVE COOKING TIME: 10-12 minutes plus standing time

SERVES: 4 people

1 head cauliflower

MORNAY SAUCE
2 tbsps butter or margarine
2 tbsps flour
1 cup milk
½ tsp Dijon mustard
½ cup grated Cheddar cheese
Salt and pepper

TOPPING
1 tbsp butter or margarine
3 tbsps dry brown breadcrumbs
Paprika

Remove all but the very pale green leaves of the cauliflower and wash well. Shake off the excess water and wrap the whole head of cauliflower in plastic wrap. Place upside down on a plate and cook on HIGH for 3 minutes. Turn over and cook an additional 3-4 minutes, or until the base is tender. Leave the cauliflower to stand, covered, for 3 minutes while preparing the sauce. Melt the butter for the sauce in a glass measure on HIGH for 1 minute. Stir in the flour and gradually add the milk. Stir continuously until the mixture is smooth. Add the mustard and salt and pepper and cook on HIGH for 1½-2 minutes, until smooth and thick. Stir in the cheese

Right: Vegetable Stir-Fry.

and leave to stand. Melt the butter for the topping for 30 seconds on HIGH and stir in the breadcrumbs and the paprika and set aside. Unwrap the cauliflower and place right-side-up in a casserole or other microwave-proof serving dish. Coat with the mornay sauce and sprinkle on the crumb topping. Heat through for 1-2 minutes on HIGH before serving.

Broccoli with Brown Butter

PREPARATION TIME: 10 minutes

MICROWAVE COOKING TIME: 13-16 minutes

SERVES: 4 people

1lb broccoli spears
6 tbsps butter

**This page: Stuffed Eggplants.
Facing page: Broccoli with Brown Butter (top) and Cauliflower Mornay (bottom).**

1-2 tsps lemon juice
Chopped mixed herbs (optional)
Pinch pepper
Flaked toasted almonds

Trim the broccoli spears to an even size and if the stalks are thick, trim them down slightly. Place in a shallow dish with the stalks to the outside and the flowerets in the center. Pour over 4 tbsps water and sprinkle lightly with salt. Cover with pierced plastic wrap and cook on HIGH for

8-10 minutes. Leave covered while preparing the butter. Place the butter in a deep glass bowl and microwave on HIGH for 5-6 minutes, or until a deep golden brown. Stir every 2-3 minutes. Skim the foam from the top as it develops. Add lemon juice to taste and the fresh herbs if desired.

This page: Stuffed Tomatoes. Facing page: Mashed Potatoes (top) and Baked Potatoes (bottom).

Add a pinch of black pepper and pour over drained broccoli to serve. Sprinkle on almonds.

Glazed Vegetables

PREPARATION TIME: 20 minutes

MICROWAVE COOKING TIME:
19-21 minutes plus standing time

SERVES: 4-6 people

2 tbsps butter or margarine
1 tbsp dark brown sugar
1-2 tbsps water or vegetable stock
2 carrots, peeled and cut into strips
2 salsify, peeled and cut into strips and/or
*   2 turnips, peeled and cut into wedges*
4oz large mushrooms, quartered
6oz button or pickling onions, peeled and
*   left whole*
Salt and pepper
2 tsps Dijon mustard
Fresh rosemary or thyme

Melt the butter in a large casserole for 30 seconds on HIGH. Stir in the brown sugar and stock and heat an additional 30 seconds on HIGH to help dissolve the sugar. Heat 2 cups water for 5-6 minutes on HIGH in a loosely covered bowl. When boiling, put in the onions and leave to stand for 2-3 minutes to loosen the peels. Drain well, peel and trim the root ends. Place the carrots, salsify and/or turnips and onions in the bowl with the butter and the sugar. Cook, uncovered, on HIGH for 2 minutes. Add the mushrooms, rosemary or thyme and a pinch of salt and pepper and mix well. Cover and cook on HIGH for 8 minutes or until the vegetables are tender. Stir in the mustard and cook an additional 1 minute on HIGH. Leave to stand for 1 minute and serve immediately.

Mashed Potatoes

PREPARATION TIME: 15 minutes

MICROWAVE COOKING TIME:
6-12 minutes plus standing time

SERVES: 4 people

1½ lbs potatoes, peeled
Salt and pepper
2 tbsps butter
4-6 tbsps milk
Pinch garlic powder

Cut the potatoes into even-sized pieces and put into a large bowl with a pinch of salt and 4 tbsps water. Cover and cook on HIGH for 5-10 minutes. Leave to stand for 5 minutes. Mash until smooth and then beat in the butter, pepper and garlic powder. Heat the milk in a small bowl until very hot, and beat into the potatoes a bit at a time (it may not be necessary to add all the milk). Serve immediately or reheat for 1-2 minutes, well covered. For a variation, cut the quantity of milk in half and add one beaten egg. Mix well and fill a pastry bag with a rosette tube. Pipe swirls of potato onto a plate covered with waxed paper. Chill thoroughly. Brush with additional beaten egg and sprinkle lightly with paprika. Cook on HIGH for 3-4 minutes until piping hot.

Baked Potatoes

PREPARATION TIME: 5 minutes

MICROWAVE COOKING TIME:
18 minutes

SERVES: 4 people

4 potatoes, 9oz each in weight
½ cup butter mixed with one of the
*   following combinations:*
1 tbsp chopped chives and 2 tsps Dijon
*   mustard*
1 tbsp chopped parsley and 2 tsps anchovy
*   paste or essence*
1 tsp chopped basil and 2 tsps tomato
*   paste*
1 clove garlic, crushed and 1 tbsp
*   crumbled blue cheese*

Scrub the potatoes well and pat them dry. Prick them 2 or 3 times with a fork and place in a circle towards the edge of the turntable. Cook for 18 minutes, turning over halfway through cooking. Wrap each potato in foil and allow to stand for 5 minutes before serving. Make a crosswise incision in the top of each potato and press at the base to open

Right: Glazed Vegetables.

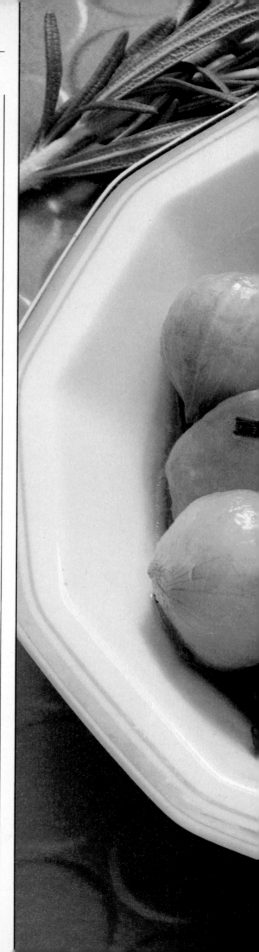

Above: Pears in White Wine and Cassis. Right: Plums in Port.

the cuts. Serve with one of the flavored butters. To prepare the butters, place the butter in a small bowl and soften for 20 seconds on HIGH. If the butter is not soft enough to mix, heat an additional 10 seconds on HIGH. Mix in the chosen flavoring ingredients and roll the butter into a cylinder shape in plastic wrap. Chill until firm and then cut into slices to serve.

Pears in White Wine and Cassis

PREPARATION TIME: 20 minutes

MICROWAVE COOKING TIME: 18-24 minutes

SERVES: 4 people

1 cup white wine
3 tbsps Creme de Cassis
½ stick cinnamon
Peel of ½ a lemon
1 cup granulated sugar
4 dessert pears, peeled

Combine the wine, cassis, cinnamon

stick and lemon peel in a deep bowl that will accommodate 4 pears snuggly. Cook on HIGH for 6-8 minutes, until piping hot. Stir in the sugar and microwave an additional 2 minutes on HIGH to dissolve. Leave the stems on the pears, but remove the eyes from the bottom of each. Place the pears stem side up. Cover the bowl with plastic wrap cutting a hole for each pear stem. This will keep the pears upright as they cook. Cook on HIGH for 10-14 minutes, or until the pears are tender. Remove the pears to a serving dish and take out the cinnamon stick and the lemon peel. If desired, the sauce may be thickened with 2 tbsps arrowroot or cornstarch before serving. Serve either hot or cold.

Honey and Brandy Peaches

PREPARATION TIME: 20 minutes

MICROWAVE COOKING TIME: 27-33 minutes

SERVES: 6 people

1 cup water
1 cup honey
1 tbsp lemon juice
4 tbsps brandy
6 ripe peaches

Place the water in a large bowl and cook for 2-2½ minutes or until hot. Stir in the honey and the lemon juice and blend well. Cook for a further 2-3 minutes, stirring every 1 minute. Remove from the microwave oven and leave to stand while preparing the peaches. Pour 4 cups water into a large bowl, cover and cook on HIGH for 8-11 minutes, or until boiling. Drop in 3 peaches at a time, and

leave to stand for 1-1½ minutes. Using a draining spoon, transfer the fruit to cold water. The skins should peel off easily. If not, repeat the procedure until the peaches peel easily. Repeat for the remaining 3 peaches and place all the peaches into the prepared syrup. Cover the bowl loosely and cook on MEDIUM for 7 minutes. Add the brandy and stir well. Leave the peaches to cool in the syrup. Serve warm or cold with whipped cream if desired.

Stuffed Tomatoes

PREPARATION TIME: 10 minutes

MICROWAVE COOKING TIME: 6 minutes

SERVES: 4 people

4 large ripe tomatoes
2 tbsps butter or margarine
1 shallot, finely chopped
8oz mushrooms, finely chopped
1 cup fresh white breadcrumbs
1 clove garlic, crushed
1 tbsp white wine
1 tsp Dijon mustard
1 tsp chopped parsley
1 tsp chopped oregano
¼ tsp thyme
Salt and pepper

Pour 2 cups water into a large bowl. Cover with plastic wrap and microwave on HIGH for 5-6 minutes, or until boiling. Place 2 tomatoes in the water and let stand for 1-1½ minutes. Remove the tomatoes to a bowl of cold water and peel off the skins. Repeat with the remaining 2 tomatoes. Remove the cores and cut the tops from the rounded ends. Scoop out the seeds, and strain the juice. Place the butter in a small bowl with the shallot and cook for 1 minute on HIGH. Add the

mushrooms, wine and garlic and cook for 2 minutes on HIGH. Stir in the breadcrumbs, mustard, herbs, seasoning and tomato juice. Mix well and fill the tomatoes with the mixture. Place the tomatoes in a circle in a shallow dish and place on the tops at a slight angle. Cook, uncovered, for 1-2 minutes on HIGH, depending upon the ripeness of the tomatoes. Serve hot and garnish with parsley if desired.

Plums in Port

PREPARATION TIME: 15 minutes

MICROWAVE COOKING TIME: 14 minutes

MAKES: Approximately 4 cups

1½ lbs plums, halved and stoned
3 cups granulated sugar
1½ cups ruby port or red wine
2 whole cloves or 1 cinnamon stick

Put the sugar and port or wine into a large, deep bowl. Put in the cloves or cinnamon stick and cook, uncovered, for 4-8 minutes on HIGH, stirring occasionally to help dissolve the sugar. Put in the plums and cover the bowl with plastic wrap and cook for 5 minutes on HIGH. Reduce the power to MEDIUM and cook a further 5 minutes. Remove the wrap and allow the plums to cool. Serve warm or cold with whipped cream or ice cream.

Facing page: Honey and Brandy Peaches.

Microwave

100 MICROWAVE SECRETS

PRESERVES AND PICKLES

Curried Fruit

PREPARATION TIME: 10 minutes

MICROWAVE COOKING TIME:
30-60 seconds plus 2-3 minutes
standing time

SERVES: 4 people

2 cups mixed dried fruit salad
2 tsps curry powder
2 tsps to 1 tbsp cornstarch
Juice of ½ a lemon
2 tbsps water

Place the dried fruit in a deep bowl.
Mix the curry powder, cornstarch,
lemon juice and water together.
Sprinkle over the fruit and cover
with plastic wrap. Cook on HIGH
for 30-60 seconds, or until the fruit is
plump and softened, stirring after
half the time. Leave to stand,
covered, 2-3 minutes. If the liquid
has not thickened enough, mix
additional cornstarch with enough
water to make a thick paste and fold
into the fruit. Cook a further
1 minute on HIGH to thicken. May
be served hot or cold with meat and
poultry.

Aromatic Oil

PREPARATION TIME: 10 minutes

MICROWAVE COOKING TIME:
1½-2 minutes

MAKES: 2 cups

2 cups vegetable oil or olive oil or a half-
and-half mixture
Peel of 1 lemon or 1 small orange
Fresh herbs such as rosemary, thyme or
tarragon

2 cloves garlic or 2 shallots
12 black peppercorns
6 whole cloves
6 allspice berries
4 juniper berries
2 bay leaves

Pour a little water into two 1 cup
bottles and sterilize for 2-3 minutes

**This page: Curried Fruit. Facing
page: Aromatic Oil (left) and
Rosemary Vinegar (right).**

on HIGH. Drain the bottles upside
down on paper towels. Choose from
the list of ingredients and divide
them equally between the two

bottles. Pour over the oil and heat the bottles for 1½-2 minutes on HIGH, uncovered. Cover and seal while still warm, and store in a cool, dark place for 1-2 weeks before using. Use in salad dressings and for sautéeing.

Pickled Orange Slices

PREPARATION TIME: 10 minutes

MICROWAVE COOKING TIME: 16 minutes

MAKES: Approximately 3 cups

3-4 oranges
1½ cups sugar
1 cup water
1 cup white wine vinegar
1 stick cinnamon
2 whole allspice berries
4 whole cloves

Slice the oranges into ¼ inch rounds, discard the ends and remove any seeds. Put the sugar, water, vinegar and whole spices into a bowl or into 2 cup sterilized jars. Cook, uncovered, for 6 minutes on HIGH. Put in the orange slices and cover with plastic wrap. Cook for 10 minutes on MEDIUM, or until the orange rind looks clearer. Remove the plastic wrap, seal and cover while still warm. Keep in the refrigerator.

Sweet Pickled Onions

PREPARATION TIME: 20 minutes

MICROWAVE COOKING TIME: 15 minutes

MAKES: Approximately 4 cups

4 cups button or pickling onions
1½ cups light brown sugar
2 cups cider, malt or white wine vinegar
½ cup water
1 tbsp mustard seed
½ cinnamon stick
Pinch salt

Put the onions in a large bowl and pour over enough water to cover.

Cook on HIGH for 1 minute. Drain and peel the onions. Put all the remaining ingredients together in a large bowl. Cook, uncovered, for 5 minutes on HIGH, stirring frequently. When the sugar has dissolved, remove the cinnamon. Put the onions in sterilized jars or into a large glass bowl. Spoon the pickling liquid over the onions and cook a further 5 minutes on HIGH. If cooked in a bowl, spoon into sterilized jars. Seal while still warm and cover. Keep in the refrigerator.

Rosemary Vinegar

PREPARATION TIME: 10 minutes

MICROWAVE COOKING TIME: 1½-2 minutes

MAKES: 2 cups

2 cups red or white wine vinegar or cider vinegar
2-4 sprigs fresh rosemary
12 black peppercorns

Pour a little water into two 1 cup bottles and sterilize on HIGH for 2-3 minutes. Drain the bottles upside down on paper towels. Place the sprigs of rosemary and the peppercorns in each bottle and pour on the vinegar. Heat, uncovered, for 1½-2 minutes on HIGH. Seal and cover the bottles while the vinegar is still warm. Leave in a cool, dark place for 1-2 weeks before using.

Three-Fruit Marmalade

PREPARATION TIME: 20 minutes

MICROWAVE COOKING TIME: 50-60 minutes

MAKES: 5-6lbs

4 limes
2 oranges
2 grapefruit
3 cups boiling water
7 cups granulated sugar

Squeeze the juice from the limes,

oranges and grapefruit and reserve. Cut away the peel and shred it thinly, coarsely or chop in a food processor as desired. Place the remaining pith and seeds into a piece of cheesecloth and tie into a bag. Place the juice, bag of pith and seeds and shredded peel into a large bowl. Add half the water and leave to stand for 30 minutes. Add the remaining water and cover the bowl with plastic wrap, piercing several times. Cook on HIGH for 25 minutes. Uncover the bowl and remove the cheesecloth bags and squeeze out the juice. Add the sugar and cook, uncovered, for 20-25 minutes or until the setting point is reached, stirring every 5 minutes. To test the setting point, put a plate into the freezer for 30 minutes. Drop a spoonful of the marmalade onto the plate and if it solidifies and wrinkles when the plate is tilted, setting point has been reached. Allow the marmalade to stand for 5 minutes. Sterilize the jars as for Aromatic Oil. Ladle the hot marmalade into the jars, seal and cover while still warm.

Rhubarb and Raspberry Jam

PREPARATION TIME: 10 minutes

MICROWAVE COOKING TIME: 13-15 minutes

MAKES: Approximately 4 cups

2 cups rhubarb, cut into small pieces (frozen or canned rhubarb, well drained may be substituted)
2 cups red raspberries
4 cups sugar
3 tbsps lemon juice
¼ cup pectin for every 2 cups cooked fruit (optional)

Put the rhubarb into a large bowl and cover with pierced plastic wrap. Cook for 2 minutes on HIGH and

Facing page: Pickled Orange Slices (top) and Sweet Pickled Onions (bottom).

add the raspberries. Re-cover the bowl and cook for 1 minute on HIGH. If using frozen or canned rhubarb, cook with the raspberries for 3 minutes on HIGH in a covered bowl. Add the sugar and lemon juice and stir well. Cook, uncovered, for 10 minutes on HIGH, stirring frequently. Measure the fruit and juice and add the necessary pectin, if using, stirring well to mix. Cook for a further 1 minute on HIGH. Test the jam by stirring with a wooden spoon. If it leaves a channel, the setting point has been reached. If not, cook a further 2-3 minutes on HIGH.

This page: Rhubarb and Raspberry Jam (top) and Three-Fruit Marmalade (bottom). Facing page: Cheesecake.

Sterilize jars as for Aromatic Oil and pour the hot jam into the jar. Seal and cover while the jam is still warm.

BAKING, DESSERTS AND BEVERAGES

Cheesecake

PREPARATION TIME: 20 minutes
plus chilling time

MICROWAVE COOKING TIME:
16-24 minutes

MAKES: 1 cake

FILLING
2 packages cream cheese
⅔ cup sugar
6 tbsps light cream or milk
Grated rind and juice of ½ a lemon
Pinch salt
4 eggs

CRUST
4oz graham crackers
3 tbsps butter or margarine
1 tbsp sugar

TOPPING
6 tbsps raspberry, strawberry or cherry
   preserve
1 tsp lemon juice

Microwave the cream cheese in a deep bowl for 1 minute on MEDIUM, or until softenend. Beat in the sugar, milk or cream and salt. Add the lemon juice and rind and the eggs gradually, beating continuously. Cook the mixture on HIGH for 4 minutes or until very hot and slightly thickened. Stir well every 2 minutes. Line a 9 inch microwave cake dish with a circle of waxed paper or 2 thicknesses of plastic wrap. Pour in the cheese mixture and leave to stand. To prepare the crust, grind the graham crackers in a food processor until fine. Cook the butter for 30 seconds-

1 minute on HIGH, pour onto the crackers and add the sugar. Process to mix and then sprinkle on top of the cheese mixture, pressing down lightly. Microwave on MEDIUM 7-15 minutes or until the cheese mixture is almost set. Rotate the dish a quarter turn every 3 minutes. A

sharp knife inserted into the center should come out almost clean when the cake is done. The mixture will firm as it chills. When completely cool, refrigerate at least 8 hours or overnight. To serve, loosen the cheesecake from the edges of the dish and carefully turn out on to a plate.

Peel off the paper or plastic wrap and set aside while making the topping. Combine the preserves with the lemon juice and heat for 1 minute on HIGH. Drizzle over the cheesecake before serving.

Hot Chocolate

PREPARATION TIME: 5 minutes

MICROWAVE COOKING TIME: 4 minutes

MAKES: 4 cups

4 tbsps sugar
3 tbsps cocoa
3 cups milk
Pinch cinnamon
4 large or several small marshmallows

Place the sugar in a large glass pitcher with the cocoa. Add ½ cup milk and mix in gradually until smooth. Cook for 1 minute on HIGH and add the remaining milk, stirring well. Add the cinnamon and cook for 3 minutes further, until hot. Pour into 4 cups and top with the marshmallows.

Bombe aux Abricots

PREPARATION TIME: 2 hours

MICROWAVE COOKING TIME: 2 minutes

SERVES: 6-8 people

1 cup dried apricots
2 tbsps brandy
1½ pints vanilla ice cream
½ cup toasted, chopped hazelnuts

Place a 4 cup bombe mold or decorative mold into the freezer for 2 hours. Roughly chop the dried apricots and place them in a small bowl with the brandy. Cover well and microwave 30 seconds to 1 minute on HIGH and set aside to cool completely. Soften 1 pint vanilla ice cream for 1 minute on HIGH. Stir in the chopped toasted hazelnuts and if the ice cream is too soft, freeze again until of a spreading consistency.

Coat the base and sides of the mold with the hazelnut ice cream and freeze until firm. If the ice cream slides down the sides of the bowl during freezing, keep checking and pressing ice cream back into place. Heat the remaining ice cream on HIGH for 1 minute or until very soft. Stir in the brandied apricots. Freeze again until slushy. Pour into the center of the hazelnut ice cream and freeze until solid. About 30 minutes before serving, unmold the bombe by briefly dipping in warm water or wrapping a hot cloth around the outside of the mold. Alternatively, if the mold is microwave-proof, heat for 30 seconds on HIGH and unmold.

Irish Coffee

PREPARATION TIME: 5 minutes

MICROWAVE COOKING TIME: 6-8 minutes

MAKES: 4 cups

2½ cups hot water
1½ tbsps instant coffee
4 tbsps Irish whiskey
6 tbsps whipped cream

Place the water in a large glass pitcher and microwave on HIGH for 6-8 minutes or until boiling. Immediately stir in the instant coffee and stir until dissolved. Add the whiskey and sugar and reheat for 1 minute on HIGH. Pour into Irish coffee glasses and top with whipped cream. Serve at once.

Lemon Meringue Pie

PREPARATION TIME: 25 minutes

MICROWAVE COOKING TIME: 14-20 minutes

MAKES: 1 pie

Right: Bombe aux Abricots.

PIE CRUST
1⅓ cups graham cracker crumbs
6 tbsps butter or margarine
2 tbsps brown sugar

FILLING
1 cup sugar
4 tbsps cornstarch
1¾ cups water
3 eggs, separated

Grated rind and juice of 1 lemon
1 tbsp butter or margarine

MERINGUE
3 egg whites from the separated eggs
1 tsp cornstarch
¼ tsp cream of tartar
6 tbsps sugar

Place the graham crackers into a food

**This page: Lemon Meringue Pie.
Facing page: Hot Chocolate (left)
and Irish Coffee (right).**

processor and work until finely
ground. Melt the butter for 30
seconds on HIGH and add to the
crumbs with the machine running.
Add the sugar and press the mixture

into a 9 inch pie dish. Cook for 1½ minutes on HIGH, rotating the dish several times. Allow to cool while preparing the filling. Combine the sugar and cornstarch with 4 tbsps water in a small bowl. When well blended, stir in the remaining water gradually. Cook on HIGH for 6-8 minutes, or until thickened and clear. Stir every 2-3 minutes. Separate the eggs and beat the egg yolks lightly. Mix a little of the hot mixture into the egg yolks and then blend the yolks into the remaining mixture. Cook on HIGH for 1 minute, stirring well. Stir in the lemon peel and juice and the butter. Allow to cool slightly and then pour into the prepared pie crust. To prepare the meringue, place the egg whites in a deep mixing bowl with the cornstarch and cream of tartar. Beat until soft peaks form. Add the sugar a spoonful at a time, beating well between each addition. Continue beating until stiff peaks form. Spread the meringue over the top of the lemon mixture, covering the filling completely. Cook on MEDIUM for 3-6 minutes or until the meringue is set, turning the dish a half turn after 1½-3 minutes. The meringue may be browned under the broiler, if desired. Refrigerate the pie until chilled and serve cold.

Steamed Raspberry Jam Pudding

PREPARATION TIME: 20 minutes

MICROWAVE COOKING TIME:
5 minutes plus standing time

SERVES: 6 people

½ cup raspberry jam
½ cup butter or margarine
½ cup sugar
2 eggs
1 tsp vanilla extract
1 cup all-purpose flour
1 tsp baking powder
2 tbsps milk

Grease a 3 cup mixing bowl or decorative mold very well with butter or margarine. Put the jam into the bottom of the mold and set aside. Cream the remaining butter or margarine and sugar until light and fluffy. Beat in the eggs 1 at a time and add vanilla extract. Sift in the flour and baking powder and fold in. If the mixture is too stiff, add up to 2 tbsps of milk to bring to a soft dropping consistency. Spoon the mixture carefully on top of the jam and smooth the top. Cover the top of the bowl or mold with 2 layers of plastic wrap, pierced several times to release the steam. Cook 5-8 minutes on HIGH. Leave to stand 5-10 minutes before turning out to serve. Serve with whipped cream or basic custard sauce.

Whole-wheat Bread

PREPARATION TIME: 1-2 hours

MICROWAVE COOKING TIME:
10-12 minutes

MAKES: 1 loaf

3 cups whole-wheat flour
1 cup all-purpose flour
1 tsp salt
1 cup milk
1 package active dry yeast
2 tbsps butter or margarine
1 tsp brown sugar

TOPPING
1 egg, beaten with a pinch of salt
Oatmeal or bran

Sift the flours and the salt into a large bowl. If topping with bran, reserve half the bran and return the rest to the bowl. Make a well in the center of the ingredients. Heat the milk for 15 seconds on HIGH. Stir in the butter to melt and the yeast to dissolve. Stir in the sugar and pour into the well in the center of the bowl and stir to incorporate gradually all the ingredients. Turn out onto a floured surface, and knead for 10 minutes. Put the dough into a lightly-greased bowl and turn over to coat all sides. Cover the yeast mixture with plastic wrap or a clean towel. Leave to rise for 1-1½ hours in a warm place. Alternatively, place the bowl of dough in a dish of hot water and put into the microwave oven for 1 minute on HIGH or 4 minutes on LOW. Leave the dough to stand for 15 minutes and then repeat until the dough has doubled in bulk. This should cut the rising time in half. Shape the dough by punching it down and kneading again lightly for about 2 minutes. Roll the dough out to a rectangle and then roll up tightly. Seal the ends and tuck under slightly. Put into a lightly greased loaf dish, about 9 inches by 5 inches. Cover the loaf dish loosely and leave dough to rise in a warm place for about 30 minutes, or use the microwave rising method. Brush the top of the loaf with lightly beaten egg and sprinkle on the remaining bran or the oatmeal if using. Cook on MEDIUM for 6-8 minutes and give the dish a quarter turn every 1 minute. Increase the temperature to HIGH and cook for 1-2 minutes, rotating as before. The top should spring back when lightly touched if the bread is done. Leave in the dish for 5 minutes before removing to a wire rack to cool. If desired, when the bread is removed from the dish, oatmeal or bran may be pressed on the base and sides.

Mulled Wine

PREPARATION TIME: 5 minutes

MICROWAVE COOKING TIME:
4 minutes, plus standing time

MAKES: 4 cups

1 pint red wine
6 tbsps sugar
2 cinnamon sticks
Rind of half a lemon
6 cloves
4 tbsps brandy (optional)

Place the wine, sugar, cinnamon sticks, lemon peel and cloves in a large bowl. Cook for 4 minutes or

Facing page: Whole-wheat Bread (top) and Fruit Scones (bottom).

until boiling. Add the brandy, if using, and leave to stand, covered, for 5 minutes. Strain and serve warm. A cinnamon stick may be placed in each cup if desired.

Spiced Orange Tea

PREPARATION TIME: 5 minutes

MICROWAVE COOKING TIME: 6-10 minutes, plus standing time

MAKES: 4 cups

2½ cups hot water
Grated rind of half an orange
3 whole cloves
1 stick cinnamon
2 tea bags

Combine the water, orange peel and spices in a large bowl. Cover and microwave on HIGH for 6-10 minutes, or until boiling. Immediately add the tea bags and leave to stand 3-5 minutes. Remove the tea bags and take out the cinnamon with a slotted spoon. Serve with the orange rind, either hot or chilled.

Fruit Scones

PREPARATION TIME: 15 minutes

MICROWAVE COOKING TIME: 3-4 minutes

MAKES: 6-8 scones

2 cups all-purpose flour
1 tbsp baking powder
4 tbsps butter or margarine
2 tbsps sugar
¼ cup golden raisins
1 egg, beaten
4 tbsps milk

TOPPINGS
1 egg white, lightly beaten
2 tbsps sugar mixed with 1 tbsp ground cinnamon or crushed graham cracker crumbs or finely chopped walnuts or toasted almonds

Sift the flour, baking powder and a pinch of salt into a large bowl and cut in the butter or margarine until

the mixture resembles fine breadcrumbs. This may be done in a food processor. Add the sugar and the raisins and stir in by hand. Stir in the beaten egg and enough milk to form a soft dough. The dough should not be too sticky. Knead the dough lightly into a ball but do not over-work. Flatten by hand or with a rolling pin to about ½ inch thick. Cut into 2 inch rounds or squares. Place the scones in a circle on a microwave baking sheet and brush the tops with

This page: Steamed Raspberry Jam Pudding. Facing page: Mulled Wine (left) and Spiced Orange Tea (right).

lightly-beaten egg white. Sprinkle with your choice of toppings and microwave on HIGH for 3-4 minutes, changing the position of the scones from time to time as they cook. It may be necessary to microwave the scones in 2 batches. Serve warm.

Creme Caramel

PREPARATION TIME: 15 minutes

MICROWAVE COOKING TIME:
24-29 minutes

SERVES: 4-6 people

CARAMEL
½ cup water
½ cup granulated sugar

CUSTARD
3 eggs
4 tbsps sugar
1 tsp vanilla extract
Pinch salt
¾ cup light cream
¾ cup milk

To prepare the caramel, place the water and sugar in a deep bowl or a glass measure and stir well. Cook on HIGH for 10-12 minutes or until golden. Do not allow the syrup to become too dark as it will continue to cook when removed from the oven. Pour into a warm 7 inch soufflé dish or deep casserole dish, tilting the dish to swirl the caramel around the sides. Allow to cool and harden completely. Beat the eggs with the sugar, vanilla and a pinch of salt until light and fluffy. Combine the cream and the milk in a glass measure and heat on HIGH for 4 minutes. Gradually add to the egg mixture, stirring continuously. Strain the mixture over the caramel, cover the dish and place in a shallow dish with enough hot water to come 1-2 inches up the outside of the custard dish. Cook on LOW for 10-13 minutes, giving the dish a quarter turn every 2-3 minutes. When a knife is inserted into the center of the custard it should come out clean when the custard is done. Do not over-cook, however, as the custard will continue to cook while standing. When cool, chill in the refrigerator for several hours. To serve, loosen the custard carefully from the side of the dish and turn out onto a serving dish. Some of the caramel will remain in the bottom of the soufflé or casserole dish once the custard is turned out. If desired, 1oz semi-sweet chocolate or 1 tbsp coffee powder may be heated

with the cream and milk and added to the custard for flavor variations.

Rhum Babas

PREPARATION TIME: 1 hour

MICROWAVE COOKING TIME:
5 minutes plus 1 minute standing time

MAKES: 12

⅔ cup milk
1 package active dry yeast
2 tsps sugar
⅔ cup butter or margarine
4 eggs
½ cup dried currants
Pinch salt

SYRUP
½ cup honey
6 tbsps water
3 tbsps brandy

Heat the milk for 30 seconds on HIGH. Mix in the sugar and yeast. Sift the flour and the salt into a large mixing bowl and warm for 15 seconds on HIGH. Make a well in the center of the flour and pour in the yeast mixture. Cover the yeast with a sprinkling of flour and leave until frothy, about 30 minutes. Stir together to form a batter. Soften the butter 30-40 seconds on HIGH and beat into the dough along with the eggs, by hand or machine. Work the dough for about 10 minutes until shiny and elastic. It will be very soft. Stir in the currants by hand. Butter 10-12 custard cups or individual molds thoroughly and spoon in the baba mixture. Cover with greased plastic wrap and leave in a warm place for 30-40 minutes. When the mixture has risen halfway up the sides of the cups, cook on HIGH for 5 minutes. The babas are done when the tops look dry. Leave to stand on a flat surface for 1 minute before turning out onto a rack. Place the honey and the water in a deep bowl and cook on HIGH for 7 minutes. Stir in the brandy and spoon the syrup over the babas to soak through. Serve with fresh fruit and cream.

Coconut Teacake

PREPARATION TIME: 20 minutes

MICROWAVE COOKING TIME:
9-11 minutes plus standing time

MAKES: 1 cake

4 tbsps butter or margarine
6 tbsps dark brown sugar
6 tbsps flaked coconut
4 tbsps chopped walnuts

CAKE
¾ cup butter or margarine
¾ cup sugar
3 eggs, beaten
1½ cups all-purpose flour
2 tsps baking powder
Milk

Line a 9 inch round cake dish with waxed paper. Place the butter in the bottom of the dish and cook on HIGH for 45 seconds-1 minute, or until the butter is melted and starting to bubble. Mix in the brown sugar, coconut and walnuts and spread evenly in the bottom of the dish. Set the dish aside while preparing the cake. Cream the butter with the sugar until light and fluffy. Beat in the eggs one at a time, beating well between each addition. Sift the flour with the baking powder and fold into the creamed mixture. Add enough milk to bring the mixture to a dropping consistency. Carefully pour over the coconut mixture in the cake dish. Cook on MEDIUM for 6 minutes, giving the dish a half turn halfway through the cooking time. Increase the setting to HIGH and continue to cook 2-4 minutes or until the cake springs back when lightly touched and begins to pull away from the sides of the dish. Let stand on a flat surface for 5 minutes before turning out onto a serving plate. Carefully remove the paper, scraping off any topping mixture and spreading it back onto the cake. Allow to cool and serve.

Coconut Teacake (top) and Rhum Babas (bottom).

Chocolate Ring Cake

PREPARATION TIME: 20 minutes

MICROWAVE COOKING TIME:
13-15 minutes plus standing time

SERVES: 6-8 people

1½ cups all-purpose flour
1½ tsps bicarbonate of soda
4 tbsps cocoa
1 cup sugar
⅔ cup butter or margarine
¾ cup evaporated milk
1 tbsp distilled white vinegar
2 eggs, beaten
Few drops vanilla extract

TOPPING
4oz white chocolate

Lightly grease a 6 cup cake ring. Sift the flour, soda and cocoa into a mixing bowl and add the sugar. Combine the evaporated milk and vinegar and set aside. Melt the butter or margarine on HIGH for 2-3 minutes or until liquid. Pour into the milk and vinegar and gradually add the beaten eggs. Pour into the dry ingredients and beat well. Pour into the cake ring and smooth down the top to level. Cook on HIGH for 10 minutes or until the top of the cake is only slightly sticky. Cool in the ring for 10 minutes then turn out onto a wire rack to cool completely. Melt the white chocolate in a small dish for 1-2 minutes on HIGH or until liquid. When the cake is cool, drizzle over the still warm white chocolate and allow to set completely before cutting the cake to serve.

Chocolate Mousse

PREPARATION TIME: 15 minutes plus chilling time

MICROWAVE COOKING TIME:
2½ minutes

SERVES: 4 people

7 tbsps unsalted butter
4 tbsps sugar
4 eggs, separated
8oz semi-sweet chocolate

4 tbsps coffee liqueur

DECORATION
Whipped cream
Coffee dragees or grated chocolate

Put the butter into a deep bowl and soften for 30 seconds on HIGH. Add the sugar and beat until light and fluffy. Gradually beat in the egg yolks. Chop the chocolate roughly and place in a small bowl with the coffee liqueur. Microwave on MEDIUM for 2 minutes or until the chocolate is completely melted. Combine the chocolate with the butter mixture and beat for 5 minutes or until the mixture is light and fluffy. Whisk the egg whites and fold into the mixture. Spoon into small dessert dishes and chill until firm. Decorate with a rosette of whipped cream and one coffee dragee or sprinkle with grated chocolate. Serve cold.

Liqueur à l'Orange

PREPARATION TIME: 15 minutes

MICROWAVE COOKING TIME:
3-4 minutes

MAKES: 3 cups

3 oranges
8oz sugar
1 pint brandy

Peel 1 of the oranges and scrape off any white pith. Set the peel aside and cut all the oranges in half and squeeze the juice. Combine orange peel and juice and sugar in a large bowl. Cook on HIGH for 3-4 minutes or until boiling. Stir frequently to help dissolve the sugar. Allow to boil for 30 seconds. Cool completely and strain the juice. Combine with the brandy and pour into a bottle. Seal well and leave to stand in a cool, dark place for 1 month before serving. Shake the bottle occasionally while storing, to mix.

Right: Chocolate Ring Cake.

Creme de Menthe

PREPARATION TIME: 10 minutes

MICROWAVE COOKING TIME:
9-10 minutes

MAKES: 2 cups

1½ cups sugar
1 cup water
6 sprigs mint or 1 tsp mint extract
Few drops green food coloring
1½ cups vodka

Combine the sugar, water and mint in a very large bowl. Microwave on HIGH 4-5 minutes or until boiling. Stir frequently to help dissolve the

This page: Eau de Framboise (left), liqueur à l'Orange (center) and Crème de Menthe (right). Facing page: Chocolate Mousse (top) and Creme Caramel (bottom).

sugar. Allow to boil for 5 minutes. Watch closely, and do not allow the mixture to caramelize. Allow to cool and then remove the mint. Add mint extract, if using, and cool. Stir in the food coloring and vodka. Pour into a bottle and seal. Leave to stand in a cool, dark place for 1 month before serving. Shake the bottle occasionally while storing.

Eau de Framboise

PREPARATION TIME: 10 minutes

MICROWAVE COOKING TIME:
7-10 minutes

MAKES: 2 cups

1lb frozen or canned raspberries in syrup
1½ cups sugar
1½ cups vodka

Cook the raspberries on MEDIUM in a large bowl for 4-5 minutes. If frozen, break up as the berries defrost. Drain the juice into a large bowl and set the raspberries aside. Stir the sugar into the juice and

microwave on HIGH for 3-5 minutes, stirring until the sugar dissolves. Allow the mixture to boil rapidly. Cool completely and then add the reserved raspberries and vodka. Pour into a bottle and leave to stand in a cool, dark place, well sealed, for 1 month. Shake the bottle occasionally to mix. Strain before serving.

Molasses Cookies

PREPARATION TIME: 20 minutes

MICROWAVE COOKING TIME:
12-18 minutes

MAKES: 24 Cookies

½ cup butter or margarine
½ cup dark brown sugar
1 egg
2 tbsps molasses
2 tsps baking powder
2 cups whole-wheat flour
Pinch salt
1 tsp allspice
½ tsp ginger

FROSTING
4 cups powdered sugar
4 tbsps hot water
Yellow food coloring (optional)
Juice of 1 lemon
Zest of 1 lemon, cut in thin strips

Beat the sugar and the butter together until light and fluffy. Gradually beat in the egg and then stir in the molasses and sift in the baking powder, flour, salt and spices. Stir together well and drop in 1 inch balls on wax paper on a plate or microwave baking sheet. Arrange in a circle of 8 balls. Cook on MEDIUM for 2-3 minutes per batch, until the tops look set. Remove with the paper and cool on a flat surface. Repeat with the rest of the mixture and when cool, remove them from the paper and place on a wire rack. To prepare the frosting, mix the powdered sugar and hot water together. Add the food coloring, if using, lemon juice and lemon zest. Once the cookies are cool, coat with the frosting and leave to set completely before serving.

Microwave Meringues

PREPARATION TIME: 15 minutes

MICROWAVE COOKING TIME:
6 minutes

SERVES: 8-10 people

MERINGUES
1 egg white
4 cups powdered sugar (all the sugar may
   not be needed)
Food colorings such as red, green or yellow
Chopped toasted nuts or sifted cocoa
   powder
Flavoring extracts
Powdered sugar
Whipped cream

Beat the egg white lightly and sift in the powdered sugar until the mixture forms a pliable paste that can be rolled out like pastry. Add chosen coloring and flavoring with the powdered sugar. The mixture may be divided and several different colorings and flavoring may be used. Roll the dough to a thin sausage shape about ½ inch thick. Cut into small pieces and place well apart on wax paper on a plate or microwave baking sheet. Flatten the pieces slightly. Cook for 1 minute on HIGH or until dry. The meringues will triple in size. Leave to cool on a wire rack. The meringue mixture may be rolled to a ½ inch thickness and a very small pastry cutter used to cut out different shapes. These meringues will be slightly larger than those made by the first method. When the meringues are cool, sandwich them together with whipped cream and sprinkle lightly with powdered sugar. Serve with a fresh fruit salad, fruit sauce or chocolate sauce, if desired.

**Right: Microwave Meringues (top)
and Molasses Cookies (bottom).**

Microwave

100 MICROWAVE SECRETS

LOW CALORIE DESSERTS

Apple Snow

PREPARATION TIME: 15 minutes	
MICROWAVE COOKING TIME: 5½-7 minutes	
SERVES: 4 people	
TOTAL CALORIES: 385	

1lb dessert apples, peeled, cored and sliced
1 tsp finely grated lemon zest
2 egg whites
2 tbsp sugar
2 drops almond extract
½ oz slivered almonds

Put the apple and lemon zest in a medium bowl, cover tightly and cook for 4-5 minutes on HIGH until pulpy. Purée in the blender. Beat the egg whites until stiff and fold half the mixture into the apple purée. Beat the sugar and almond extract into the remaining beaten whites. Half-fill four sundae dishes with the purée and pile the mallow on top. Arrange the dishes in a circle in the microwave and cook uncovered for 1½-2 minutes on HIGH until the mallow puffs up. Sprinkle with slivered almonds and quickly brown at a 6 inch distance from a hot broiler.

Rhubarb, Orange and Strawberry Comfort

PREPARATION TIME: 5 minutes	
MICROWAVE COOKING TIME: 10-12 minutes	
SERVES: 4-6 people	
TOTAL CALORIES: 202	

1lb canned rhubarb, cut into 1 inch lengths
¼ tsp ground ginger
1 10½ oz can mandarin orange segments in natural juice
Liquid sweetener
2 tbsp low fat natural yogurt
6oz strawberries, halved and rinsed
2 tbsp crunchy muesli

Put the rhubarb in a large bowl, add

This page: Rhubarb, Orange and Strawberry Comfort (top) and Apple Snow (bottom). Facing page: Hot Fruit Salad Cups.

the ground ginger and strain in the juice from the mandarin oranges. Cover and cook for 10-12 minutes on HIGH, stirring twice during cooking until the rhubarb is mushy. Mix in

sweetener to taste. Stir in the yogurt and fold in the orange segments, cover and leave to cool. Reserve four strawberries for decoration and thinly slice the remainder. Mix the sliced strawberries into the rhubarb, then spoon the mixture into individual goblets. Just before serving, sprinkle with the muesli and top with a half or whole strawberry.

Tipsy Berries

PREPARATION TIME: 5 minutes

MICROWAVE COOKING TIME:
7 minutes plus chilling

SERVES: 4-6 people

TOTAL CALORIES: 408

2 tbsps sugar
1 cup sweet red wine
2 tbsps tequila
Low calorie sweetener
1lb raspberries
4oz blackcurrants } or use all
4oz redcurrants   } blackcurrants

Mix the sugar and the wine in a medium bowl and cook uncovered for 2 minutes on HIGH. Stir until the sugar is dissolved. Cook uncovered for 5 minutes, then stir in the tequila and add liquid sweetener to taste. Trim and rinse the fruit and place in a serving bowl, then pour the syrup over. Chill thoroughly in the refrigerator, stirring occasionally.

Hot Fruit Salad Cups

PREPARATION TIME: 10 minutes

MICROWAVE COOKING TIME:
6½ minutes

SERVES: 4 people

TOTAL CALORIES: 457

2 large oranges
2 tbsps sugar
1 tsp rum
1 small dessert apple
1 slice fresh or canned pineapple
1 banana
¼ oz shelled pistachios, skinned and
   chopped

Halve the oranges and put in a shallow dish, cut side down. Cook uncovered for 2 minutes on HIGH until the juice can be easily squeezed. Gently squeeze the juice and scrape out most of the flesh. Set the shells aside. Stir the sugar into the juice and cook uncovered for 1-1½ minutes on HIGH until boiling. Stir, then cook uncovered for 2 minutes on HIGH. Add the rum. Core and cube the apple, cut the pineapple into wedges and peel and slice the banana, and mix all the fruit into the juice. Cook uncovered for 30 seconds on HIGH, then stir and cook for a further 30 seconds on HIGH. Spoon the fruit into the orange shells and pour the syrup over. Decorate with pistachio nuts.

Blackberry and Raspberry Molds

PREPARATION TIME: 5 minutes

MICROWAVE COOKING TIME:
7 minutes plus setting time

SERVES: 4 people

TOTAL CALORIES: 290

8oz fresh or frozen blackberries
8oz fresh or frozen raspberries
Approximately 1 cup fresh orange juice
2 tbsps cold water
2 tsp gelatin
Liquid sweetener
4 rosettes whipping cream

Put the blackberries in one bowl and the raspberries in another and cook each separately, uncovered, for 3 minutes on HIGH or until the juice runs freely. Strain the juices into a wide-necked jug and make up to 1¼ cups with the orange juice. Put the water into a small dish or glass and cook for 30 seconds on HIGH until hot but not boiling. Sprinkle the gelatin over the surface and stir thoroughly. Cook for 20 seconds on HIGH, then stir until the gelatin is completely dissolved. Leave to cool for a few moments before pouring into the fruit juices. Stir in liquid sweetener to taste. Chill until just

beginning to set. Divide the blackberries between four tall glasses and cover with the juice. Refrigerate until set, then top up with the raspberries. Decorate each with a rosette of cream.

Home Made Yogurt

PREPARATION TIME: 5 minutes

MICROWAVE COOKING TIME:
12-13 minutes plus setting time

MAKES:
approximately 2½ cups

TOTAL CALORIES: 262

2 cups skimmed milk
4 tbsps skimmed milk powder
4 tbsps low fat yogurt

Put the milk in a large bowl and cook uncovered for 2 minutes on HIGH. Stir and cook for a further 2-3 minutes on HIGH until the milk boils. Reduce the setting and cook uncovered for 8 minutes on DEFROST (35%), stirring occasionally until the milk is slightly reduced. Whip in the milk powder and leave to cool until comfortable to the touch. Whip in the yogurt, then pour into a wide-necked flask or divide between the glasses in a yogurt maker. Cover and leave for 8 hours until the yogurt is just set, then refrigerate covered for a further 3-4 hours.

Chocolate Creams

PREPARATION TIME: 5 minutes

MICROWAVE COOKING TIME:
5 minutes plus chilling time

SERVES: 4 people

TOTAL CALORIES: 568

¼ cup cocoa powder, sifted
⅓ cup custard powder
2½ cups skimmed milk

Facing page: Home Made Yogurt (top) and Tipsy Berries (bottom).

Low calorie sweetener
1 milk coated chocolate Graham cracker, grated

Mix the cocoa and custard with a little of the cold milk in a medium bowl. Whip in the remaining milk and cook uncovered for 5 minutes on HIGH, whipping frequently until thickened. Add sweetener to taste. Divide the cream between four individual molds and leave to cool for 30 minutes, then cover with plastic wrap and refrigerate until cold. Remove the plastic wrap and decorate the tops of the creams with grated cracker.

Coffee Soufflés

PREPARATION TIME: 20 minutes

MICROWAVE COOKING TIME: 40 seconds

SERVES: 4 people

TOTAL CALORIES: 795

½ cup double strength hot black coffee
1 tbsp powdered gelatin
2 eggs, separated
2 tbsp sugar
¾ cup canned evaporated milk, well chilled
½ tsp vanilla extract
1 small bar dairy flake chocolate, finely crushed
4 rosettes whipping cream

Cut four strips wax paper and attach to four individual custard cups with an elastic band, making sure that the collars protrude 1 inch above the rims. Put half the coffee in a medium jug and heat uncovered for 30 seconds on HIGH. Sprinkle on the gelatin and stir to dissolve. If necessary return to the microwave for a further 10 seconds. Beat the egg yolks and sugar until thick and mousse-like. Beat in the remaining coffee, then mix in the dissolved gelatin. In another bowl whip the milk and vanilla extract until very thick, then fold into the coffee mixture. Leave in a cool place until on the point of setting, then beat the egg whites until stiff and fold into the mixture. Pour evenly into the prepared dishes and chill until set. With the aid of a round-bladed knife dipped into hot water, remove the paper collars. Decorate the soufflés with crushed, flaked chocolate and a cream rosette.

This page: Blackberry and Raspberry Molds. Facing page: Chocolate Creams (top) and Apple and Cherry Sponge Cakes (bottom).

and vanilla extract together until thick. Fold in the flour and the chopped apple. Divide the mixture between approximately fifteen double thickness paper cases and sprinkle the cherries over each. Arrange five at a time in a circle in the microwave and cook for 45 seconds to 1 minute on HIGH until the cakes are just dry on top. Do not overcook.

Baked Bananas Sauce au Poire

PREPARATION TIME: 15 minutes	
MICROWAVE COOKING TIME: 6 minutes	
SERVES: 4 people	
TOTAL CALORIES: 375	

1 large orange
2 ripe pears
Low calorie sweetener
4 small bananas

Pare thin strips of orange and shred finely. Put into a jug, cover with cold water and cook on **FULL POWER** for 2 minutes or until tender. Drain and set aside. Halve the orange and squeeze the juice of one half into a blender. Remove and chop the segments from the remaining half of orange and set aside. Peel, core and cut up the pears, and blend with the orange juice to a smooth purée, adding sweetener to taste. Peel the bananas and put into a small dish. Cook uncovered for 2 minutes on HIGH, then reposition the fruit, placing the two outside bananas into the middle. Pour the pear purée over the bananas and cook uncovered for 2 minutes on HIGH. Top with the chopped orange and decorate with the reserved shreds. Serve immediately.

Apple and Cherry Sponge Cakes

PREPARATION TIME: 15 minutes	
MICROWAVE COOKING TIME: 2-3 minutes	
MAKES: approximately 15	
TOTAL CALORIES: 590	

2 large eggs
Pinch cream of tartar
2 tbsps sugar
½ tsp vanilla extract
½ cup all-purpose flour, sifted
1 dessert apple, peeled, cored and finely chopped
⅛ cup candied cherries, finely chopped

Beat the eggs, cream of tartar, sugar

This page: Coffee Soufflés. Facing page: Baked Bananas Sauce au Poire.

Microwave

100 MICROWAVE SECRETS

INDEX